WALLACE-HOMESTEAD
PRICE GUIDE TO

AMERICAN
Country
ANTIQUES

TENTH EDITION

DON & CAROL RAYCRAFT

WALLACE-HOMESTEAD
PRICE GUIDE TO

AMERICAN *Country* ANTIQUES

TENTH EDITION

DON & CAROL RAYCRAFT

Wallace-Homestead Book Company
Radnor, Pennsylvania

Library of Congress Catalog Card No. 86-640023
ISBN 0-87069-550-9

Designed by Anthony Jacobson
Cover photograph taken at Joseph & Peter Country Antiques, Berwyn, Pennsylvania

Manufactured in the United States of America

1 2 3 4 5 6 7 8 9 0   9 8 7 6 5 4 3 2 1 0

To our good friends
Joe and Opal Pickens
of Watseka, Illinois,
whose encouragement,
knowledge, friendship,
and front door
have always been
open to us

Immigrant's box, originally from Norway, blue exterior and red interior, mid-nineteenth century. **$350–$500**

Contents

Shaker milk keeler, painted finish, finger lap construction, pine staves, nineteenth century. **$600–$750**

Acknowledgments

Joe and Opal Pickens
Gary and Susan Sheets
Jo Ann Garrett
Father Tom Pincelli
Patrick and Christine
  Francomano
David and Marie Oldred
Lezlie Colburn
Armando and Emedelia Juarez
Alex Hood
Michael Fallon of Copake
  Country Auctions
Joy and Robert Luke of Joy
  Luke Auction Gallery
Jimmie L. Ghere
Arthur Bartges

Terri and Joe Dziadul
Steve Rhodes
Pat Newsom
Creekside Antiques
Ellen Tatem
Rose Holtzclaw
Lancaster, Kentucky, Antique
  Mall
Patricia McDaniel
Old Storefront Antiques
John and Mary Purvis
Nathan and Mary Price
Gerry and Bernie Green
Jamie Eckert
W. F. Katona

PHOTOGRAPHY

Carol Raycraft
R. Craig Raycraft
Joe Dziadul
Ellen Tatem

John Purvis
John C. Fairval
Kyle C. Schiebel
Mark Harper

Introduction

Factory-made metal spice box, original gold paint and black lettering on drawers. **$400–$500**

In the 1960s and 1970s there were several guide-books written that described to collectors the best places to find American country antiques in quantity and at affordable prices. Today collectors are only occasionally finding country antiques in quantities and only rarely at affordable prices. Consequently, it takes a great deal more time, knowledge, and money now to be a collector than it took only a decade ago. The diminishing supply of American antiques and rapidly rising prices and interest have combined to change the rules. There are now "serious" collectors from Maine to California and at most rest areas in between. This great interest in collecting antiques brings with it some changes. For example, in the 1950s and 1960s it was difficult to make a mistake concerning authenticity because there were relatively few people interested in painted cupboards, dry sinks, and pie safes, and thus there was minimal profit to be made in the construction of fakes. Back then, people were more likely to be taking paint *off* a piece of country furniture than "moving it around" or re-placing it, as is the situation today.

A collector from the distant past, M. L. Blumenthal, presented his recommendations for successful antiques shopping in the February 16, 1924, issue of *The Saturday Evening Post.* At that point there were not many individuals looking for country furniture. Blumenthal's message to potential collectors of Windsor chairs, highboys, gate-leg tables, and cherry candlestands was based on his 10 years of traveling along the eastern seaboard from his home near Philadelphia. Blumenthal wrote:

There is just so much genuine old stuff available, and the supply is not being increased: at least we like to think it is not. Ten or twenty years ago people sold century and more old furniture as they now sell worn-out golden-oak or mission, for what it would bring, or wring, from the secondhand dealer. "My, my," our middle-aged visitors tell us, "You paid sixty dollars for that piece? I remember when we refurnished our home in 1905 or was it 1906? We gave at least twenty pieces like that to our ashman's wife." And they did.

Much of the kind of antiques situation Mr. Blumenthal described in 1924 is equally true today, though the cast of characters on most "want to buy" lists has changed. Imagine a great warehouse in the sky where discarded furniture goes to wait its turn to become collectible. The "worn-out golden-oak and mission" that Blumenthal dismissed to the secondhand shops in 1924 for whatever it would "bring or wring" has been working its way to the top of a lot of collector's lists over the past 15 years. The pieces that have survived the ashman's wife and the secondhand dealer are valuable and are constantly rising in price.

The fact that golden-oak furniture was mass-produced in the late nineteenth and early twentieth centuries has little bearing on current values. The golden-oak and mission pieces were relegated to the imaginary warehouse until the stack of items in front of them in line to be collected was almost gone. Then interest began to grow as the people who wanted "antiques" suddenly found oak to be somewhat readily available and still affordable.

Golden oak was produced in huge quantities for furniture stores across America. Between 1880 and 1910 it could be purchased almost anywhere two roads came together. Blumenthal noted in 1924 that it had no value. Today it has significant value and can be found almost anywhere. A collector today in Cheyenne is almost as likely to find a claw-footed table as a traveling salesman from St. Louis at an antiques mall, backyard auction, or shop in Syracuse.

Blumenthal did not describe dry sinks, cupboards, or blanket chests in 1924 because no one cared about such items. However, after the supply of highboys and Windsor chairs began to dwindle, collectors looked at "country" furniture in a more favorable light.

We have now reached the point that great cupboards, tables, and pie safes are still available, but there are few bargains. If a collector wants a significant piece, he or she must expect it to be expensive.

Average country collectors who are short of time and money are beginning to have serious problems finding pieces at prices they can pay. Such collectors may be forced to look in a different direction for purchases—maybe they can find a relative of the ashman's wife who hasn't sold all the stuff she was given after the other guy refurnished his house in 1905 or 1906.

Blumenthal's 1924 *Saturday Evening Post* article, called "Antiqueering," included some key words and phrases for his readers who were going to follow him into the wilds in search of antiques. Many of the terms he selected as being important to collectors almost 70 years ago are equally critical today in understanding the complexities of the antiques business. Blumenthal's terms are as follows:

client: an individual who buys easily and pays without comment

copy: a reproduction

customer: an individual who constantly haggles for a better price or chooses not to buy

dog: a poorly made and fairly modern piece

fake: a spurious piece

"find": a piece you have an opportunity to buy for much less than its value

"in the rough": a piece in its original condition

junk: something that the buyer is trying to purchase at a discounted rate

"museum piece": an item a seller is trying to sell

restored: repaired

stuff: collective term for antiques

Trends

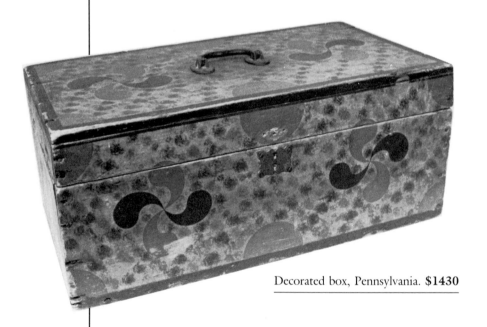

Decorated box, Pennsylvania. **$1430**

In recent years there have been major changes in the way most collectors buy antiques. Particular pieces that we previously tripped over in shops and at shows have all but vanished, and prices have risen to heights that leave seasoned collectors astonished.

General Trends

The "trends" that we list below are not limited to a single geographic area but are national in scope.

Trend 1. There is a growing tendency for collectors of American country antiques to find a fairly stable price structure at shops and shows from Maine to California. A painted sugar bucket or firkin in Maine that is priced at $225 ($200 to a dealer) may be offered in California for $265 ($250 to a dealer). This relative consistency is a departure from the pricing situation of a decade ago when there were much greater geographic disparities in pricing. The increasing interest nationally and the diminishing supply of quality goods have brought about this change.

Trend 2. The quality of merchandise in many antiques malls continues to decline as the number of malls grows. The malls that are interested in longevity tend to monitor the quality of their dealers' merchandise. For example, if such a mall allows crafts, the crafts are restricted to a separate area and not commingled with the antiques and collectibles.

Some malls are increasing the size of their dealer booths so that furniture and accessories can be displayed in room settings rather than stacked on top of each other.

A general-line antiques mall allows dealers to display items ranging from Windsor chairs to carnival glass and baseball cards. They may limit what is offered to antiques and collectibles and prohibit "new" items, but they are not concerned about a specific period or type of merchandise.

Trend 3. Cooperative shops run by a combination of participating dealers specializing in a particular category or period of antiques, which have been prominent in the east for a decade, have in recent years been a growing factor in the midwestern and west coast antiques world. The number of such cooperative shops will continue to grow as concerns about the quality of malls increase.

Trend 4. Prices for quality items in original condition also will continue to increase significantly as the already limited supply of such items decreases and the number of collectors grows. The most dramatic price jumps will take place as individual pieces of country furniture are classified as "folk art" and a different kind of collector enters the marketplace.

In the early 1970s we collected Shaker boxes, baskets, and furniture and paid several hundred dollars for items that routinely sell for several thousand today. The price structure

changed because "Shaker" was discovered by a new species of collector, the members of which operate at a different level and from a much more complex mind-set than do other collectors. Unquestionably, the same kind of interest is springing up for most American country antiques.

In October 1989 we attended a highly promoted antiques show in Elmhurst, Illinois. The emphasis of the show was Americana. On the way out we noticed an exceptional pine dry sink with its original coat of red paint. Ten years ago it might have been priced at $750, which many people would have thought was much too expensive. This example was marked $3900, and no one seemed too surprised.

Trend 5. We pointed out above that prices are tending to become more "national" than regional. A side note to that trend is that unusual pieces are turning up almost anywhere and are bringing serious dollars at auction.

In late July 1989 the Time Was Museum near Mendota, Illinois, was sold at public auction. We had driven by the museum on Route 51 numerous times and never stopped. A 7-foot tall statue of an American eagle, chip-carved by Albert Halberg out of catalpa wood, sold for $66,000. Below the eagle were carvings of George Washington, Abraham Lincoln, the American flag, and several Indians. (Halberg died in 1949, and the statue had eventually been put on loan to the museum.)

Trend 6. As the interest in painted and original surfaces increases, collectors are gradually beginning to discriminate and are becoming more selective about the pieces they purchase. A pie safe in "as found" condition with traces of paint and damaged tins may be good enough for the cover of *Country*

Living, but it should not necessarily be a part of a collection of painted furniture.

Trend 7. On occasion two different groups of collectors compete for the same items, causing prices to soar. For example, in recent years there has been a national mania for baseball-related "antiques" (collectibles). Any advertising or tobacco container or sign with a baseball-related logo or scene has increased in value several times over the past few years. As a result, advertising collectors have been forced to pay much higher prices for such items than they had paid in the past.

Folk art collectors have shown much more interest in decorated stoneware and painted furniture recently than ever before. Prices of superior examples of stoneware and painted furniture have risen significantly at shops, shows, and auctions as the competition intensifies.

Price Trends

An auction can serve as a barometer of price trends and collector interests across the nation or in a limited geographic area.

The listings that follow include selected auctions from several time frames. It is interesting and informative to look back at prices and auctions from the recent past to better understand the market for Americana today.

Stewart Gregory Collection of American Folk Art and Furniture, January 27, 1979, New York, New York

1. Rare molded copper "Columbia" weathervane, American nineteenth century, height 31", $12,000
2. Life-top chest, New England, 1810–1840, painted and grained, $3750
3. Portrait of two children by William Matthew Prior (1806–1873), oil on board, painted c. 1830, $13,000
4. Fine molded zinc figure of George Washington, American, nineteenth century, height 58", $3250
5. Carved and painted wood figure of a gentleman, American, nineteenth century, height 18", $2400
6. Important carved and painted wood bust of Capt. M. Starbuck, Nantucket, 1838, height 13½", $30,000
7. Extremely fine and rare carved and painted wood figure of a racetrack tout, attributed to Charles Dowler, Providence, Rhode Island, c. 1870, height 6' 4", $29,000
8. Portrait of a child by John Brewster, Jr. (1766–1854), oil on canvas mounted on aluminum, $67,500 (record for a Brewster and the highest priced item in the sale)
9. Fine, rare molded and gilded copper Indian weathervane, American, nineteenth century, height 28", $17,000
10. Set of six thumb-back side chairs, Cape Cod, Massachusetts, 1820–1840, original freehand and stenciled decoration on a yellow background, fine condition, $1000

Danville, Pennsylvania, Stoneware Auction, April 1989

1. Four-gallon jug, Cowden and Wilcox, Harrisburg, Pennsylvania, cobalt cornucopia, $7000
2. Eight-gallon churn, White and

Wood, Binghamton, New York, floral decoration, two minor rim chips, $4800

3. Five-gallon jug, W. Hart, Ogdensburg, New York, slip-trailed horse's head, $3100

4. Five-gallon churn, Rochester, New York, Burger Jr., shorebird in a marsh, rim repair, $2600

5. Four-gallon jar, Bennington, Vermont, double bird singing on a branch, $1525

6. M. Woodruff six-gallon double-handled jug, Cortland, New York, double flower on the front, blue handles, single flower on the back, mint, $1000

7. Two-gallon jug by White's of Utica, New York, fantail bird on a branch, minor chip, $475

8. One-gallon jug, J. & E. Norton, Bennington, Vermont, bird on a twig, "spider cracks," $250

9. Two-gallon ovoid jar with "1831" in blue cobalt, cracked, $210

10. Three-gallon jug, brushed decoration and stenciling, William & Reppert, Greensboro, Pennsylvania, $165

11. Three-quart batter pail with a fern and leaf decoration, ear missing, $120

12. Four-gallon churn, E. W. Farrington & Co., Elmira, New York, triple floral decoration, minor rim chip, cracked, $395

13. Three-gallon crock, leaf decoration, N. A. White & Son, Utica, New York, minor rim chips and spots of discoloration, $175

14. Two-gallon F. Stetzenmeyer, Rochester, New York, leafy plant with flowers, minor glaze flakes, $600

15. Three-gallon butter or cake crock, cobalt decoration, 13″ diameter, chip on bottom edge, $500

16. Four-gallon crock, Cowden and Wilcox, Harrisburg, Pennsylvania, bold bunch of grapes, blue on handles, four minor cracks, $625

17. Three-gallon advertising or vendor's jug, Phelan & Donahue Wholesale Liquors, 67 John St., Utica, New York, $120

Robacker Auction, May 27–28, 1989, Lancaster County, Pennsylvania

Cookie cutters:
Fireman, $200
Indian girl, $775
Uncle Sam, $3000
"Runaway Slave," $7400

Chalkware:
Pocket watch holder, $1600
Canary, $230
Pair of lovebirds on a pedestal, $650
Reclining ram, $250
Squirrel, $650
Large parrot on a ball on a pedestal, $400

Stoneware:
J. B. Pfaltzgraff and Company, York, Pennsylvania, one-gallon crock with slip-trailed decoration of a woman walking a dog on a leash and exclaiming "Oh my!", in deep cobalt, $19,000
Batter jug with bail handle, Cowden and Wilcox, "man in the moon" brushed decoration, $10,000

Shaker Auction, August 6, 1989, Pittsfield, Massachusetts

1. #7 rocking chair with taped seat and back, $990

2. #0 child's rocking chair, $1650

3. #6 armed rocking chair, $1100

4. Chrome yellow oval box, 2½" high, 3½" long, 2½" deep, with a pincushion on its cover, $8800
5. Framed string bean label, $275
6. Red painted blanket chest, $2200
7. Shaker seed box, replaced lid, Mt. Lebanon label, $1540

Auction of Wallace Nutting Pictures, Books, and Furniture, September 8–9, 1989, Danbury, Connecticut

During the first quarter of the twentieth century, Wallace Nutting marketed mass-produced prints that were found in most middle-class American homes. Nutting followed in the business footsteps of Currier and Ives, who had been equally as successful during the nineteenth century.

Nutting (1861–1941) had a business that produced and sold hand-colored photographic prints of New England homes and scenes. The more than 2500 different prints were sold inexpensively by the hundreds of thousands in department stores, drugstores, gift shops, and from Nutting's studio.

The peak period of sales was between 1915 and 1925. After 1930 the market for Nutting's work diminished annually until his death in 1941.

The rarest and most collectible of the Nutting prints are snow scenes, children, animals, men, cows, and seascapes. Scenes that contain men and children are especially sought after by Nutting collectors. These subjects are usually listed under "Miscellaneous Unusual Designs" when Nutting's works are cataloged.

Some prices follow. Note that the prices listed do not include the 10 percent buyer's premium.

1. "A Warm Spring Day," 15" × 22", several dozen sheep graze near a lakeside, $210
2. "The Maple Sugar Cupboard," 14" × 17", girl reaches into a cupboard by a fireplace, $110
3. Wallace Nutting's biography, first edition with dust jacket, $75
4. "A Berkshire Road," 12" × 20", stony brook bends around orchard and rail fence, $65
5. "Summer Wind," 10" × 12", rippling pool surrounded by a stone wall and flowers, $45
6. "Pine Landing," 10" × 12", canoe rests under tall pine tree, $70
7. Bow-backed Windsor chair, #302 bow-backed Windsor with block "Nutting" signature, $425
8. "A Divining Cup," 10" × 12", girl in orange dress has tea in formal setting, $130
9. *Pennsylvania Beautiful,* second edition book with original dust jacket, $30
10. "The Apple Tree by the Stream," 11" × 14", blossom tree rises above a stream, $50

The 1670 Tavern Antiques, East Haverhill, Massachusetts, April 1957 Price List

1. Round eagle butter stamp, nicely carved, $10
2. Carrier for hot coals, metal tray, wood handle, $4
3. Log mortar, 18" high, with pestle, dug to point, $9
4. Staved rum keg (*see* Gould Plate 108), $15
5. String of 29 sleigh bells on metal links, $7.50
6. Small covered redware jar, glazed inside, $1.50

7. Fine tin candle sconce, tipped hood, 13", $12.50
8. Oval tin candle mold, six-tube, (1–4–1)
9. Tin candle mold, four-tube, trays both ends, $4.50
10. Pennsylvania Dutch smoothing board, 1702, decorated, $40
11. Cookie roller with fish, fern, rabbit, $6
12. Magnificent round burl bowl, 17½" diameter, $37.50

Copake Country Auctions

Michael Fallon is an auctioneer and appraiser who conducts cataloged Americana auction sales of formal and country furniture, Shaker pieces, quilts, coverlets, hooked rugs, samplers, and folk art. Mr. Fallon's business, Copake Country Auctions, is a member of the National Auctioneers Association, New England Appraisers Association, International Society of Appraisers, and the Columbia County Chamber of Commerce. The pictures that follow are items sold recently at auction by Mr. Fallon.

Copake Country Auctions
Box H
Copake, NY 12516
(518) 329-1142

Step-back cupboard, early nineteenth century. **$2200**

Child's Empire chest. **$440**

Step-back cupboard. **$1100**

Cupboard, early nineteenth century. **$1980**

French-Canadian country chest, eighteenth century. **$880**

Tiger maple bed. **$1980**

Shaker revolving stool, Mt. Lebanon, New York. **$3550**

Signed and dated tramp art server, Pennsylvania. **$500**

Birth record from 1826. **$3900**

Pennsylvania fraktur signed by "Umble." **$3300**

Tramp art box with mirror. **$650**

Pennsylvania fraktur, 1797. **$1900**

Sampler signed "Helen Harrower," dated 1846. **$600**

Miniature bureau box attributed to John Webber of Lancaster, Pennsylvania, dated 1846. **$3400**

Amish cart. **$525**

Doll carriage signed Richardson and McKees, patent date of 1873. **$275**

Hooked rug by contemporary artist Nina Moore Elvey (Pennsylvania). **$330**

Grouping of New England hollow-cut silhouettes, c. 1820. **$4950**

Signed Nina Elvey hooked rug. **$500**

Decorated box, Pennsylvania. **$1430**

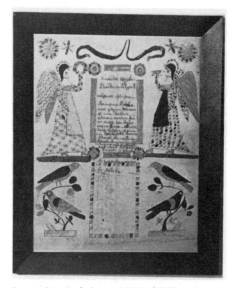

Pennsylvania fraktur, 1843. **$550**

Pennsylvania fraktur attributed to the Reverend Henry Young, dated 1821. **$6380**

Whimsical tramp art. **$575**

Silk sampler quilt. **$1980**

Cora Bates, oil painting on a wooden panel. **$1150**

Shaker five-finger box, 13½″ × 9½″ × 6″. **$4180**

Framed paper cutting or "scherenschnitle," Pennsylvania. **$300**

Painting from the Walter P. Chrysler collection. **$2100**

Watercolor depicting fruit. **$850**

Tailgate from a buckboard. **$385**

Shaker seed box, **$1300–$1600;** Shaker pickle bottle, **$325–$400.**

Seed boxes, late nineteenth century: **$225– $250, $325–$375, $275–$325.**

Seed boxes from the mid-nineteenth century. **$375–$475** each

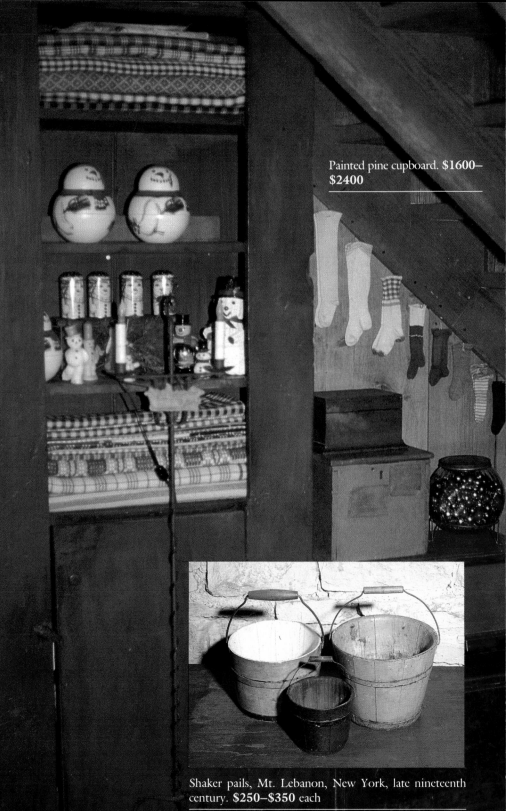

Painted pine cupboard. **$1600–$2400**

Shaker pails, Mt. Lebanon, New York, late nineteenth century. **$250–$350** each

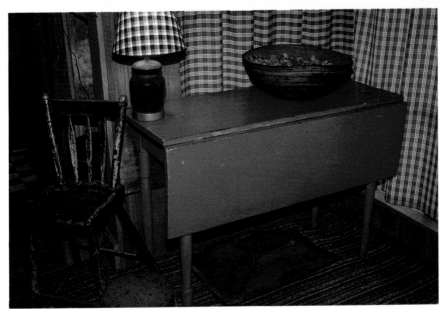

Pine drop-leaf table, c. 1850. **$750–$950**

Collection of redware pottery. **$100–$400** each

Rockingham molded pitcher, c. 1875. **$275–$325**

Stoneware coffeepot and coffee mug, midwestern, early 1900s: pot, **$225–$275;** mug, **$100–$125.**

Stenciled and brush-decorated jar, Greensboro, Pennsylvania. **$650–$750**

Five-gallon "bird" jug. **$450–$525**

Rooster windmill weight, Elgin, Illinois, early 1900s. **$700–$900**

Stoneware cake crock. **$425–$525**

Painted dry sink, late nineteenth century. **$1300–$1700**

Noah's ark c. 1900. **$550**

Game board signed "A.L.," dated 1914. **$275**

Work of John Bechtel, c.1903. **$3630**

Miniature portrait, Daniel Tenmier, eighteenth century. $577

24

Family record of the Dickinson family, Gloucester, Massachusetts, 1787–1816. **$880**

"Cobweb" quilt, 84″ × 100″. **$770**

Cast iron hitching post without base. **$550**

Signed Roger Bourgault carving. **$220**

Pennsylvania folk art, nineteenth century. **$3630**

Albany, New York, stove dated 1845. **$1100**

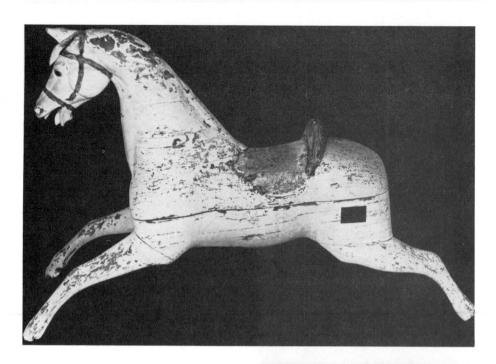

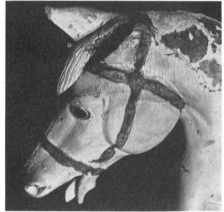

Carrousel horse. **$1375**

Folky carved lion cane. **$575**

Wirligig. **$1430**

Sampler quilt, 80″ × 88″. **$880**

Log cabin quilt, 83″ × 88″. **$605**

29

Taconic friendship basket, mint condition. **$520**

N. Currier, "Pleasure" and "Vexation." **$300** pair

Hudson River landscape in the style of Thomas Cole, 46″ × 69″. **$4400**

Unsigned painting. **$3750**

Silk log cabin quilt, 87″ × 85″. **$715**

Silk needlework. **$412**

Appliqué quilt with sprays of "stuffed" berries, 78″ × 80″. **$990**

"Stars" quilt, 84″ × 83″. **$2200**

Princess feather appliqué quilt, 93″ × 94″. **$990**

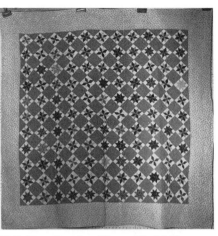

"Mini stars" quilt, 63″ × 65″. **$440**

Hepplewhite slant-lid desk. **$3700**

Centennial furniture: candle stand, **$605**; tambour desk, **$990**.

Six figured maple side chairs, signed "Seymour, 1862, Troy, N.Y." **$891** set of six

Hudson Valley Kas, early green paint, c. 1740. **$4950**

Eighteenth-century bucket cupboard. **$797**

Connecticut River Valley high chair from the Florine Maine collection. **$2420**

New Hampshire birdseye maple chest, c. 1810. **$1237**

Eighteenth-century Hudson Valley pewter shelf. **$2090**

Queen Anne lowboy (some restoration). **$2200**

Eighteenth-century demilune table. **$880**

Single-drawer tavern table. **$1760**

Oak rolltop desk, 54", signed "T. G. Sellew, 111 Fulton Street, New York". **$1650**

Eighteenth-century desk on frame. **$2750**

Grain painted two-drawer blanket chest. **$1760**

English fireside settle, pine. **$715**

Joy Luke Auction Gallery

The Joy Luke Auction Gallery is an auction and appraisal company that conducts estate and consignment catalogued auctions and specialized sales throughout the year featuring estate jewelry, Indian artifacts, dolls, toys, textiles, and furniture. The Joy Luke auctioneers are members of the National Auctioneers Association and the Illinois State Auctioneers Association.

Joy Luke's commission is 20 percent, and all items are fully insured. No buyer's premium is charged. Catalogs, mailing lists, and additional information may be secured by contacting

Joy Luke Auction Gallery
300 E. Grove Street
Bloomington, IL 61702
(309) 828-5533

Comb-back armchair, **$200**; quilt with squares and stars, **$160**.

Blue-and-white earthenware soup plate, **$70**; Wood and Son blue-and-white historical plate, **$275**.

Framed oil on canvas depicting child holding kitten, 14″ × 17″. **$500**

Victorian parlor lamp decorated with hollyhocks. **$250**

Child's cast iron stove, "The Favorite." **$850**

Toy fire pumper truck. **$650**

Nick Klein child's rocking horse with horse-hide covering. **$850**

Disney "Disneyland Ferris Wheel." **$140**

Disney "Mickey Mouse" tin toy watering can. **$290**

Keystone "Mickey Mouse" toy projector. **$575**

Pair of Bennington-type lidded jars, **$275**; Bennington-type jelly mold, **$90**.

Collection of early metal toy banks: (*top*) **$175, $425, $150, $1075**; (*bottom*) **$100, $175, $80, $50**.

Early cast-metal toy cart with horse and driver. **$475**

Ideal novelty toy, "Ferdinand the Bull." **$180**

Brite tin toy Coca-Cola delivery truck with bottles. **$375**

Schoenhut "Felix the Cat." **$225**

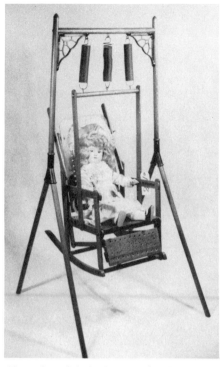

Glascocks oak baby jumper. **$360**

Blue stoneware syrup jug. **$500**

Collection of miniature lamps: (*top*) **$400, $225, $200, $175**; (*bottom*) **$175, $500, $80, $120**.

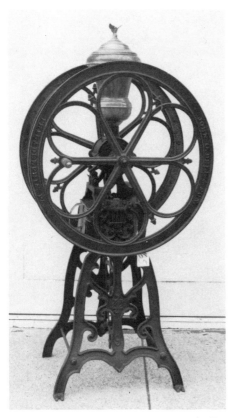

Large John C. Dell and Son #9 coffee grinder. **$425**

Wicker tea cart with glass tray. **$150**

Signed Alfred Montgomery oil on canvas. **$3800**

Apache Indian coil basket. **$1200**

Royal Bonn China case clock. **$525**

"End of the Trail" table lamp. **$350**

Tiffany 10-shade water lily lamp. **$12,400**

Eagle campaign torch. **$2300**

Royal Bayrueth sunbonnet babies porcelain tray. **$330**

Fisher Price wooden pull toy, "Mickey Mouse Band." **$750**

Oval reversible educational board. **$85**

"Little Boss" wooden toy pull cart. **$625**

Louis Marx "Amos 'n' Andy Fresh Air Taxicab." **$1400**

Ives toy train set. **$1150**

Structo red tin toy fire pumper truck with six ladders and brass fixtures. **$850**

Early tin horse and cart. **$375**

Doll with parasol, porcelain head. **$180**

Four procelain dolls: **$175, $175, $325, $275**.

Hanging cranberry glass lamp. **$750**

CHAPTER TWO

Collecting American Antiques a Century Ago

Bail-handled pantry box, painted finish, factory-made. **$200–$225**

In the late nineteenth century, newly made furniture was much more expensive to purchase than were "antiques" or "relics" from the 1740–1840 period. The "old" furniture had been stored in barn lofts or outbuildings and forgotten. Books by Clarence Cook and Charles Locke Eastwood were a major force in transforming a large group of Americans of moderate means into intentional collectors of such furniture.

Many people who left the heat of the city each August to travel to their rustic cabins in the mountains furnished their vacation homes with American antiques because such pieces were cheap and plentiful. Others ordered Adirondack furniture, made locally from twigs and branches, to add to the rustic look of their summer retreats. Adirondack furniture has again come into favor among collectors in the 1990s, and prices have rapidly escalated as the interest in the "northwoods," or rustic, look has returned.

Wealthier Americans purchased European antiques because they were expensive and somewhat difficult to obtain. The Arts and Crafts Movement of the late nineteenth and early twentieth centuries brought additional changes to the home furnishings industry. The quality of Arts and Crafts furniture was high, and the materials were carefully selected and utilized by skilled craftsmen. Furniture made with such care and quality was a direct contrast to the mass-produced "colonial revival" furniture of the 1880s, which offered several combinations of periods in a single piece, indifferent craftsmanship, and inferior materials.

Collector's Chronology

1870s Several eastern collectors are gathering and displaying "relics" (pieces of furniture and other items) that belonged to famous Americans of the eighteenth century.

1872 Englishman Charles Locke Eastwood writes *Hints on Household Taste,* an influential book that changes interior design in the United States.

1876 The Centennial Exposition is held in Philadelphia and spurs interest in Americana.

1878 American Clarence Cook writes *The House Beautiful* and encourages people to furnish their homes with American antiques in a "tasteful" manner.

1880s American antiques begin to have status as home furnishings rather than having importance only because of some patriotic or historical association. As the home becomes more of a focus for decoration and good taste, many middle-class people begin to accumulate affordable American antiques. A period of "colonial revival" begins with mass-produced "early American" furniture made inexpensively and quickly and sold in most furniture stores east of the Mississippi River.

1890s Numerous New England collectors are searching for antiques from the eighteenth and early nineteenth century. The collectors find that "antiques" are less expensive than new home furnishings.

1891 Irving Lyon writes *Colonial Furniture of New England.*

1892 Alice Morse Earle's *China Collecting in America* is published.

Country
Furniture

Refinished walnut corner cupboard
found in Ohio, paneled doors, c. 1850.
$1600–$2000

The market for painted furniture is continuing to grow, and prices are rising accordingly. It is difficult to find a painted cupboard, bed, pie safe, or dry sink that has maintained the quality of its original finish enough so that any serious collector can take it from a show, shop, mall, or market and put it directly into his or her home. Most painted furniture is offered in "as found" condition directly out of a basement, barn, or attic, or off a back porch. The piece may be structurally sound, but in most cases exposure to the elements has taken a toll on the painted surface and desirability over the years.

As prices continue to rise for furniture with a painted finish, the temptation for repainting, enhancing existing paint, or blatant faking grows. Some individuals cannot resist turning a $750 refinished pine cupboard into one with its "original" painted finish and a $2750 price tag. Thus, when buying painted furniture a collector should always closely scrutinize the finish and ask many questions about the piece and its condition before writing a check.

An excellent source of painted furniture is often collectors who are disposing of their holdings due to death, divorce, or disinterest. A dry sink or cupboard that had been purchased in the 1960s or 1970s for a few hundred dollars may now be worth a few thousand. The collector who can triple his or her $300 investment from 1970 is usually pleased, as is the buyer who can obtain a quality piece for a sum below existing market prices.

Buying Country Furniture

Before you write the next check for country antiques, study the steps below very carefully.

1. Take the time to examine a piece of furniture closely. Do not buy it emotionally. Step back and give it an intellectual appraisal. Let the piece convince you that it is "right."

2. Look for scribe and score marks and any signs of repair. Pay special attention to nail holes that have no reason for being on the piece or in a particular place.

3. Be concerned if the back of a cupboard you are considering has been painted. Often this is done to cover up obvious construction flaws or reworkings and replacements.

4. Rarely will a piece of country furniture be signed by its maker. Check for the unlikely event of the maker's signature or mark on the underside of a chair seat or the back of a cupboard.

5. The kinds of wood used in the construction of the piece of furniture are important. Country dry sinks and cupboards through much of the nineteenth century were very rarely made of oak. Pine, poplar, and walnut were usually the woods of choice. Maple is used by Ethan Allen and Tell City today, but it was not commonly found on nineteenth-century American country furniture other than on chair legs.

6. The finish of a piece of furniture is a primary determinant of its value. It is not uncommon to find several pieces of furniture with questionable paint and hefty price tags at even the most prestigious antiques shows.

If you have the slightest question about the age of a painted finish, hire a second opinion or don't bring the piece home. If you are not sure about the authenticity of the piece when you write the check, you will question it for as long as you own it. Make it a point to have the dealer indicate on any receipt that the piece has its original or old finish.

Be aware that as prices rise and the interest in painted surfaces increases, the quality of the paint jobs on old furniture will be improved.

7. The provenance, or history of ownership, of a piece of furniture is a complex area of concern. How can you trace the path of a cupboard from the 1830s to the present? If there is a house across the street from you that was constructed in 1837 with a huge cupboard in an upstairs bedroom that requires a wall being taken out to remove the cupboard, then you have a nearly positive provenance for the cupboard because it has probably been in place since the house was built. However, few attempts at assembling probable provenance for a piece are that clear-cut in the real world.

Dating Country Furniture

A careful inspection of a piece of country furniture can provide some insights into its age that a casual observer might miss. The information below offers a general dating process than can be valuable in making such an inspection.

Circular saw marks: after 1850

Milled lumber without plane marks: after 1875

Machine-made dovetails: after 1890

Scribe marks on drawers for dovetails: before 1890

Score marks on chair legs and posts for locating rungs and slats: before 1850

Wooden pins: before 1850

Blown glass with bubbles, wavy lines: before 1850

Gimlet or pointed heads on screws: after 1865

Hand-forged hinges: before 1825

Cast iron butt hinges: after 1830

Wooden "mushroom" knobs, 1″ deep: after 1825 until well into the twentieth century

Pressed-glass knobs: after 1825

Machine-cut threads on screws: after 1830

Irregularly shaped nuts: before 1860

"Signed" furniture: most country furniture that is "signed" predates 1840

The Etiquette of Buying Country Antiques, or How to Act Like a Pro

There are some basic courtesies that antiques consumers should know about and put into operation while visiting shops, malls, and shows. Many of these courtesies are obvious, but others are a little more subtle.

Dealers are often infuriated by the apparent ignorance of their customers. Most dealers encourage questions about their merchandise and usually are very helpful. However, the following statements are typical of many that dealers face in their shops or at shows and represent the kind of approach that should be avoided by collectors:

"We threw out two exactly like that when my _____ died."

"Hell, I got one at home that I'd sell for a *lot* less than that."

"I'll give ya $_____ for it."

"When I was a kid I paid only a dime for one of those, and they can't be worth that much more now."

"We go to the flea market every Sunday down at the American Legion and I saw one of them blue cupboards for $75 last week."

Where *Not* To Shop

There are a multitude of "how to" books that tell you the correct procedures for buying wine, real estate, art, stocks, pickles, and so on. Each is written by an expert who will save you trouble, time, and money if you follow his or her guidelines.

Over the years we have established a few simple rules for buying country antiques. If you do business with anyone who violates these rules, don't say you haven't been warned. We will not buy antiques in a shop where:

An elderly woman with a cigar says "The carnival glass is here and the primitives is in the shed."

You find wet paint on your hand after you touch a cupboard with its "original" finish.

The dry sinks and pie safes are made of plywood.

A piece of furniture that is described as "untouched, right out of an 1830 house" has pink paint.

The owner has more blue cupboards in his shop than teeth in his mouth.

The Tale of a Dry Sink

To demonstrate various aspects of the antiques business, we here trace the trail of ownership of a hypothetical pine dry sink from the moment it leaves the storage space in a barn or attic until it is carefully carried into someone's front room.

1. A dry sink with three coats of paint and a missing door is brought out of a southern Indiana barn and sold at a closing-out farm sale.

2. A local "picker" buys the sink for $50 and loads it on his truck.

3. The picker offers it to two area dealers for $175 the next day. They choose not to buy it because of the repairs it needs and because stripping the sink requires too much labor.

4. The picker sells the sink for $150 to a dealer at a Sunday antiques market in a nearby town.

5. The dealer spends $110 to have the old door replaced and $100 to have the old paint "taken down" to the base coat of red. The replaced door is painted to match the old red paint.

6. The sink is offered for $575 with a notation on the price tag that a door has been replaced and the paint matched.

7. A suburban dealer in country antiques visits the shop and buys the sink for $517.50 ($575 less a 10 percent discount).

8. The sink is priced at $875 at a three-day show in Indianapolis. The tag does not indicate that the door is a replacement. The code on the tag reads #1432–D800.

9. A young couple buys their first piece of country furniture with its "original" painted finish for $875 plus applicable sales tax.

10. If they would have asked "Is that the best that you can do?" they probably could have bought the dry sink for the "dealer's price" of $800.

In a period of about six weeks the dry sink has already passed through at least four pairs of hands. It is not difficult to appreciate why provenance can be a major problem.

Most antiques dealers can take the piece back no farther than the person from whom they acquired it. The suburban dealer who sold the sink to the young couple can only tell them that it was purchased from another dealer in central Indiana.

Shaker rocking chair, Mt. Lebanon, N.Y., late nineteenth century, #7 size. **$1200–$1600**

Boston rocking chair, spindle-back, stenciled crest rail, factory-made, c.1875. **$350–$425**

Ladder-back rocking chair used for sewing or nursing, replaced woolen taped seat, original painted finish, late nineteenth century. **$175–$225**

Ladder-back rocking chair, replaced rush seat, refinished, c. 1850. **$250–$300**

Painted ladder-back rocking chair, splint seat, c. 1850; found in Kentucky. **$300–$350**

Set of six arrow-back side or dining chairs, factory-made, painted finish, 1860–1880. **$1500–$2000** set of six

Unusual youth or high chair, pine, painted original finish, c. 1920. **$135–$150**

Windsor spindle-back chair, saddle seat, New England, c. 1840. **$600–$850**

Mammy's bench with gate to hold child, stenciled crest rail, arrow-back, mid-nineteenth century. **$1200–$1500**

Half-spindle-back side or dining chair, stenciled saddle seat and crest rail, factory-made, original decoration, c. 1875, **$200–$240**; set of six, **$1800–$2200**.

Ladder-back side chair, replaced splint seat, unusual finials, painted finish, late nineteenth century. **$150–$175**

Lodge hall or dining chairs, factory-made, painted finish, late nineteenth century or early twentieth century: one chair, **$50–$65**; set of six, **$350–$400**.

Half-arrow-back side or dining chair, painted finish, 1850–1875, **$125–$150**; set of six, **$800–$1200**.

Child's chair, spindle-back, factory-made, overpainted, early 1900s. **$45–$55**

Four half-spindle-back dining chairs, painted finish with decorated crest rail. **$800–$1000** set of four

Windsor side chair, spindle-back, saddle seat, painted finish, c. 1840. **$600–$700**

Arrow-back side chair, painted finish, 1860–1875, **$135–$150**; **$750–$900** set.

Child's ladder-back arm chair, original painted finish, 1830–1850. **$375–$450**

Painted footstool, "half moon" ends, late nineteenth century. **$90–$115**

Pine jelly cupboard, painted, c. 1870. **$900–$1300**

Painted arrow-back youth chair, mid-nineteenth century. **$175–$225**

Pine bench, probably used on a back porch, original unpainted condition. **$75–$95**

Painted step stool, early twentieth century. **$250–$300**

Painted spindle-back bench, maple and pine, probably used in a train depot, c. 1900. **$500–$700**

Painted pine bench, moritised top, "half moon" ends, found in Vermont, c. 1880. **$250–$350**

Six-foot pine bench from a rural central Illinois church, c. 1900. **$250–$325**

Painted bucket bench, dovetailed top, c. 1850. **$500–$600**

Oak and ash wardrobe, factory-made, early twentieth century. **$500–$600**

Refinished pine cupboard, late nineteenth century. **$700–$800**

Top of two-piece cupboard offered for sale as a jelly cupboard, pine, replaced wire front, mid-nineteenth century. **$325–$375**

Walnut and pine pie safe, turned legs, c. 1880. **$900–$1200**

Unusual painted cupboard with paneled doors, late nineteenth century. **$1500–$1850**

Pine jelly cupboard with "bootjack" legs, painted finish, c. 1870. **$800–$1200**

Country wardrobe, pine, painted finish, un-usual bracket base, mid-nineteenth century. **$1200–$1500**

Maple storage cabinet, factory-made, refin-ished, c. 1900. **$300–$375**

Refinished walnut corner cupboard found in Ohio, paneled doors, c. 1850. **$1600–$2000**

Step-back cupboard, painted finish, pine, c. 1880. **$1200–$1600**

"As found" pine cupboard, probably has lost some height at base and needs to be refinished, c. 1850, **$550–$650**; refinished, **$750–$1100**.

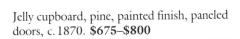

Jelly cupboard, pine, painted finish, paneled doors, c. 1870. **$675–$800**

Pine corner cupboard, paneled doors, "blind" front, c. 1860. **$2200–$2500**

Step-back pine cuboard, painted finish, paneled doors, mid-nineteenth century. **$1500–$2000**

Jelly cupboard, painted pine, original finish, 1860–1880. **$675–$850**

Partially stripped jelly cupboard, pine, 1850–1880: **$600–$675** as found; **$800–$925** refinished.

Grained chimney cupboard, mid-nineteenth century. **$1300–$1500**

Crude country pine cupboard, white paint, early 1900s. **$575–$650**

Jelly cupboard with tin panels, walnut, 1860s. **$850–$1000**

Painted pine pie safe with star tins, single drawer below, 1860–1880. **$1200–$1500**

Pie safe, painted finish, mid-nineteenth century. **$900–$1200**

Unusual pie safe with pierced doors, turned legs, and paneled sides, c. 1850. **$2000–$2400**

Overpainted pie safe, pine, mid-nineteenth century, **$700–$800** as found; **$1200–$1400** stripped to base coat of paint.

Pie safe with 12 pierced tins, pine, mid-nineteenth century. **$600–$800**

Stripped pine cupboard with pierced tin upper doors, 1870s. **$700–$850**

Pine cupboard with tin sides, paint of indeterminate age, 1860–1880. **$500–$700**

Simple painted pie safe, pine, mid-nineteenth century. **$500–$600**

Rare pie safe on legs, probably from Pennsylvania, pine, painted finish, c. 1840. **$1300–$1700**

"As found" pie safe, overpainted, pine, great flower tins in doors, c. 1860. **$750–$850**

Unusual apothecary chest with 14 drawers, painted finish, replaced drawer pulls, late nineteenth century. **$1400–$1600**

Leather-covered factory-made trunks, late nineteenth century. $75–$95 each

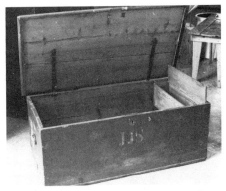

Pine chest, painted with initials "JJS" on front, till, c. 1840. **$575–$650**

Dome-top immigrant's chest dated 1852, pine, original painted finish. **$500–$600**

Jelly cupboard with new screen wire inserts in doors, pine, c. 1880. **$400–$500**

Twelve-drawer apothecary chest, original painted finish, pine, c. 1900. **$330–$385**

Unusual meal or grain bin, painted pine, late nineteenth century. **$385–$425**

"As found" 15-drawer chest painted pine, original finish, paneled sides, c. 1875. **$1500–$1750**

Painted grain bin, pine, paneled front and sides, turned feet, c. 1880. **$500–$600**

"As found" small bin, half-moon cutouts on sides, crackled paint, pine, twentieth century. **$55–$70**

Storage bin possibly for bread, "as found" condition, painted wood, early twentieth century. **$100–$125**

Refinished pine dry sink, replaced copper lining, probability of lost height on base, c. 1880. **$450–$500**

Three-drawer chest, paneled sides, turned legs, c. 1880. **$225–$300**

Unusual eight-drawer chest from a general store, original condition but lettering has faded, c. 1900. **$225–$275**

Four-drawer walnut chest, factory-made, c. 1880. **$300–$350**

Painted four-drawer chest with drop-lid writing surface, 1875–1885. **$600–$700**

Child's chest of drawers, refinished, factory-made, early 1900s. **$75–$100**

Painted and grained chest of drawers, 1880–1900. **$300–$400**

Sugar chest, turned legs, painted pine, c. 1850. **$335–$400**

Child's bed, bold finials, turned legs, c. 1850. **$350–$400**

Painted pine three-legged table, late nineteenth century. **$150–$225**

Oak icebox, factory-made, c. 1900. **$500–$575**

Pine hutch table with storage area under seat, painted and grained, rare form, c. 1850. **$3000–$4000**

Painted pine desk, c. 1880. **$250–$325**

Pine side or tavern table, painted finish, c. 1850. **$600–$700**

Painted softwood box, early 1900s. **$150–$175**

Pennsylvania desk-on-frame, dovetailed corners, stenciled decoration, c. 1830. **$900–$1300**

Factory-made drop-front desk, oak and ash, early 1900s. **$200–$240**

Maple and pine desk, "as found" condition, c. 1880. **$350–$450**

Crude child's cradle, painted pine, nailed sides, early 1900s. **$100–$150**

Doll cradle, walnut painted red, heart cut-out, Pennsylvania origin, c. 1830. **$300–$350**

Painted pine doll cradle, nailed sides, c. 1900. **$125–$150**

Unusual dry sink with wainscotted front, painted pine and poplar, early 1900s. **$500–$650**

Farmhouse table, "scrubbed" top, pine, painted base, c. 1880. **$450–$550**

Kitchen and Hearth Antiques

This chapter, prepared by Teri and Joe Dziadul, illustrates items from their personal collection. The Dziaduls have been filling special requests for more than 20 years and offer a lengthy list of kitchen and hearth antiques to collectors and dealers. The current list may be obtained by sending $1.00 to 6 South George Washington Road, Enfield, Connecticut 06082.

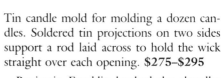

Tin candle mold for molding a dozen candles. Soldered tin projections on two sides support a rod laid across to hold the wick straight over each opening. **$275–$295**

Benjamin Franklin loathed the chandler trade, as revealed in his autobiography. At the age of 10 Franklin was taken from school to assist in his father's business: "I was employed in cutting wick for the candles, filling the dipping mold, and the molds for cast candles, attending the shop, etc."

In eighteenth-century America, most families lived on small farms. Virgin lands were cheap, but backbreaking labor was necessary to bring them into cultivation. Well-managed farms yielded ample food, grains from the fields, and vegetables and herbs from the kitchen garden. In the wilderness there abounded wild fruits and berries. Blackberries, blueberries, raspberries, and mulberries were eaten fresh or stewed. Above all there were strawberries, "fine and beautiful strawberries, four times bigger and better than ours in England," according to Captain John Smith. Out of the farm came milk to be drunk, churned into butter, or pressed into cheese. In the pasture, sheep provided lamb and fleece to be woven for warm winter clothing. On the farm or closeby were waters to fish and woods to hunt. The ocean yielded quantities of cod, affectionately known as Cape Cod turkey. In the kitchen, about the only bought supplies were salt, spices, molasses, cane sugar, and, for occasional inspiration, a demijohn of New England rum. The Yankee farmer learned to cultivate the black honey bee and slashed the sugar maples for sweetening to pour over his hasty pudding.

Open fireplace or "down hearth" cooking was the manner in which our ancestors prepared their meals. Meat was roasted on a dangle spit or jack rack. This required assistance, and perhaps the name "jack" relates to the custom of calling a boy or attendant by the name of Jack. By the end of the eighteenth century, tin roasting ovens proved popular and convenient. The meat could be observed and basted through the small door that lifted at the back. The curved bottom caught the juices, and one end had a spout from which juices were poured when the meat was done. Many are seen today at inns where guests can still enjoy their meat prepared in this way.

Game birds were roasted in smaller ovens, hung by the breasts, their juices caught in the base with a raised edge. A down-hearth toaster used for bread and meats was found on early hearths and came in many designs.

The built-in brick oven and "tin kitchen" turned out johnnycake, roasts, pudding pies, and cakes of delicate lightness and tantalizing flavor. Brick-oven pork and beans must have been invented early, for Judge Samuel Sewall, one of the greatest of American diarists, mentions a stop he made at Andover in 1702, "and there din'd on pork and beans."

Long-legged skillets were thrust into the hot coals of maple for cooking griddlecakes and frying meats. Heavy black iron pots yielded New Englanders their dinners for more than 200 years. Bean porridge and fish stews were daily bills of fare. Clam chowder that so enraptured Ishmael in Herman Melville's Moby Dick was standard fare along the New England coast: "But when that smoking chowder came in, the mystery was delightfully explained. Oh! Sweet friends, hearken to me. It was made of small juicy clams, scarcely bigger than hazel nuts, mixed with pounded ship biscuits and salted pork cut up into little flakes! The whole enriched with butter and plentifully seasoned with pepper and salt . . . we despatched it with great expedition."

Each year we are somewhat staggered by the dramatic price jumps that occur in our collecting area. A uniform pricing structure prevails among all experienced sellers. With such a sophisticated marketplace, much patience and wide travel are necessary to hope to find the promise of a bargain. Flea markets still attract flocks of bargain hunters with high hopes of unearthing a wonderful treasure.

Baker's sign, gilded finish, fully dimensional. **$1600–$1800**

Wooden shop sign, hung outdoors to call attention to services or goods offered for sale; painted yellow, blue, and black. **$2500–$2800**

Gilt bee skep, perhaps a fraternal organization's or beekeepers' symbol, wood, 16″ high. **$1200–$1500**

Black hawk weathervane, copper with verdigris patina, highly desired version, mid-nineteenth century. Many collectors use vanes in interior design. **$1300–$1500**

Gathering basket, ash splint, shallow depth, early 1900s. **$175–$195**

Oak splint hip basket, also referred to as an apple-gathering basket or, more commonly, a seed-sowing basket. This basket would have had a canvas lining and a leather strap. **$250– $295**

Swing-handled ash-splint apple basket, painted red. Utility baskets are more valuable if they have their original paint. **$475–$500**

Covered splint storage basket, Maine Indian, c. 1920. **$225–$275**

Butter mold, square with four individual blocks. Made by a woodenware manufacturer, this mold was probably distributed by a dairy supply house on special order. **$150–$195**

Butter stamp showing profile of a Civil War soldier. The head stock spindle is still attached to the knob. Perhaps made to order, this may be the only known example. Without other examples available to determine a market value, individual specimens such as this can sell for prices beyond the imagination. Estimated value is **$800–$1000**.

Butter stamps: eagle with star, **$375–$425**; anchor, **$475–$550**; eagle with wreath border, **$575–$625**.

Butter stamps: crowing rooster with star and moon in sky and barn in background, **$500–$575**; horse, **$950–$1100**; crowing rooster, **$495–$550**.

Cylinder butter molds (found primarily in New England): 1-lb. cow print, **$350–$395**; 2-lb. strawberry design, **$175–$195**; 1-lb. pineapple print, **$125–$145**.

Wrought iron andirons, made by blacksmith, eighteenth century. **$245–$295**

Gooseneck andirons, wrought iron, made by blacksmith, late eighteenth century. **$225–$295**

Brass andirons, log stops, Boston maker stamped on iron log rest, mid-nineteenth century. **$995–$1195**

Tin kitchen. These roasting ovens are often found without a spit rod. The rod has several slots for skewers. A turkey was thrust through the spit and secured with skewers in the spit slots. Extra-large size, **$375–$400**

Bird roaster, tin. Small birds like bobwhite or quail hung on the hooks as the roaster stood before the fire. Tin reflecting shield flips over to roast reverse side of birds. **$275–$295**

Footwarmer, oversize but not quite double (could have been used by mother and child). Metal coal holders were filled with coals from the hearth and placed under lap robes for warmth during a sleigh ride. **$475–$525**

Toddy warmers, placed on hot coals on the hearth to warm the toddy: tin, wood handle, pewter knob, larger than most, **$275–$295**; tin, wood knob, folding handle which tucks into unit, **$275–$295**.

Ale shoes: all copper, **$395–$425**; tin with lid, **$450–$495**. These slipper-shaped warmers were thrust into the hot hearth coals to mull beer or ale.

Crane, on which pots and kettles were hung over the hearth, **$575–$675**; iron kettle with brass cover and handle, **$250–$275**.

Longfellow's poetry described many old customs, and on one occasion the poet attended a wedding in East Greenwich, Connecticut, and wrote the following in a letter to his friend Mr. J. O. Field: "In one of the rooms was a tea kettle hanging on a crane in the fireplace—so begins a new household."

Tin and copper food mold, very rare example. Cucumbers, figs, and leaves surround the mold; the bottom is hinged on each end and is removable. **$400–$450**

Tenth-anniversary top hat. In the last half of the nineteenth century, Americans chose the tenth anniversary as an occasion to throw a large and hilarious party. **$900–$1000**

Teddy bear chocolate mold, 11″ high (rare size), padded paws. **$1250–$1450**

Father Christmas chocolate mold, 20″ high, rare subject and size. **$2800–$3000**

Tin candle mold for molding a dozen candles. Soldered tin projections on two sides support a rod laid across to hold the wick straight over each opening. **$275–$295**

Benjamin Franklin loathed the chandler trade, as revealed in his autobiography. At the age of 10 Franklin was taken from school to assist in his father's business: "I was employed in cutting wick for the candles, filling the dipping mold, and the molds for cast candles, attending the shop, etc."

Sugar cutter in box. Loaf or cone sugar is broken up with iron sugar cutter, and pieces are received in drawer. **$250–$295**

Patented carrot grater, paper label intact: "Patent improved Cylinder Thribble Cut Carrot Grater. Mfd. and sold wholesale and retail by A. Gilford, Ashfield, Mass. Pat. May 1867. Improved Dec. 1869." **$375–$425**

Hand cookie cutter. **$250–$295**

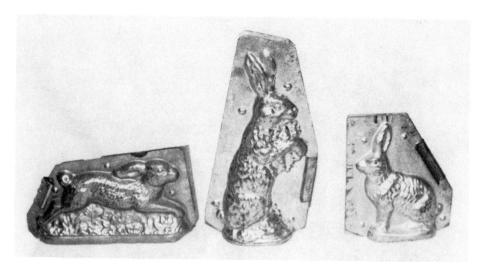

Rabbit chocolate molds: running rabbit, **$65–$75**; standing rabbit eating vegetable, **$75–$85**; sitting rabbit, **$30–$35**.

Tin cookie cutters, birds and roosters. **$75–$125**

Cookie cutter, rider on horse, large size, fine tinsmithing. **$795–$895**

Large cookie cutter, man on horse, **$1200–$1400**. Large cookie cutters have stimulated much interest lately, and record-breaking prices have been set for unusual subjects and sizes.

Grain-painted boxes, all with original hardware: (*top*) mustard yellow and reddish-brown sponging, **$825–$895**; (*center*) gray and black smoke decoration, **$625–$695**; (*bottom*) red and brown design, **$725–$795**

Tin cookie cutters: running horse, **$150–$175**; pig, **$200–$250**.

Tin cookie cutters: man figure, **$150–$175**; woman figure, **$150–$175**.

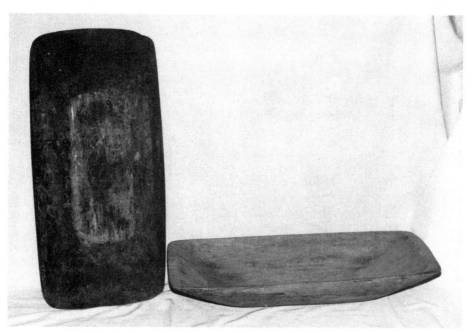

Painted wooden bowls: blue-green paint, **$250–$295**; red paint traces, **$200–$250**.

Painted wooden firkin and pail: deep blue paint on firkin, fine condition, late 1800s, **$400–$450**; oyster white pail, **$85–$95**.

Maple bowl, 15″ in diameter. **$125–$175**

Painted red bowl, 28" in diameter. Bowls of this size are not common, and the condition is very good. **$550–$650**

Cookie board depicting two young pugilists, c. 1850. These boards were pressed onto the cookie dough to create a design. **$375–$395**

Wooden cake board, goat and dog carving, used for ornamentation of little cakes. The design was made by placing the mold face-down on the dough and using a rolling pin to press it in. **$450–$495**

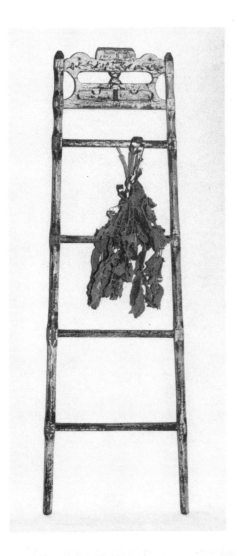

Norwegian box. This type of box is known as a tine both in Norway and in America. This is a wonderful large example with finely executed fingers and yellow and black painting on a salmon red background. **$1200–$1400**

Painted wooden herb drying ladder, scarce. **$300–$325**

Rosemaled Norwegian boxes: box dated 1858, **$650–$695**; scrolled box, **$550–$595**.

Norwegian bentwood box. Lid is fastened by a snap closure.

Between 1820 and 1915, 800,000 Norwegians emigrated to America. The immigrants brought many items with them, but the rest of the things they needed had to be made from available American woods (such as pine, walnut, and butternut). Norwegian folk art objects in America now appear in auctions and estate sales, mainly in Wisconsin, Minnesota, and Iowa, areas in which the immigrants settled in great numbers.

Pair of Mason decoys, original paint. **$600–$650** pair

Hanging pipe rack, chip carving, "SEAN CRESE MARIE BONIOVRNA 1741" carved at bottom. **$650–$695**

Wooden cheese grater, iron handle. **$125–$175**

Painted wooden shovel. Many wooden shovels have been painted with scenic folk art themes. They are prized for their aesthetic appeal. **$475–$500**

Painted bowl with traces of red paint, **$250–$295**. These large bowls must be studied to determine their use. For example, marks will be found in chopping bowls, and a bleached appearance will be found in bowls used for pouring milk in to allow the cream to rest or used to hold rising bread. Plaster fruit, **$12–$35**.

Chopping bowl and knife: bowl (very few found in this size), **$250–$275**; knife, horn handle, **$175–$200**.

Tin rolling pin used with tin pastry sheets, wooden handles. **$300–$350**

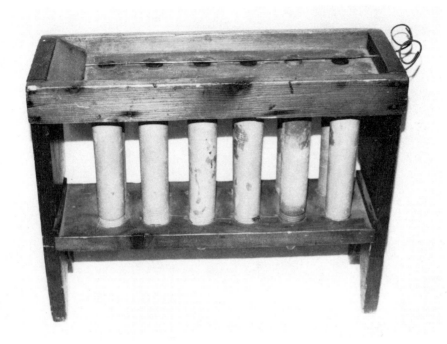

Framed wooden candle mold, redware tubes, signed "Wilcox, N.Y." **$1500–$1600**

Turned wood chandelier with delicately turned hub, wire arms, wooden candle cups, and orignal green paint; eighteenth century. **$1200–$1400**

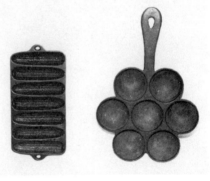

Iron cornbread and muffin pan: cornbread pan for mini corn sticks, c. 1920, **$65–$75**; three-footed cannonball iron pan for down-hearth baking of muffins, early nineteenth century, **$225–$250**.

Tin rolling pin and tin pastry sheet. **$550–$595**

Pewter match safe and tasters: match safe, **$275–$295**; mini tasters, **$35–$45** each.

Candle mold and tallow skimmer: three-tube candle mold, **$125–$145**; tin skimmer with wood handle, **$275–$295**.

Nutmeg graters: cylinder graters, **$55–$75**; flat-back graters, hand-punched, **$55–$75**; box grater with slide cover, **$75–$85**; combination nutmeg grater, pie crimper, and can opener, **$250–$275**; hand-painted grater with decoration, **$150–$175**.

Tin nutmeg graters, all made by hand (not manufactured): (*left*) **$120–$130**; (*center*) painted blue, red, and white, **$275–$295**.

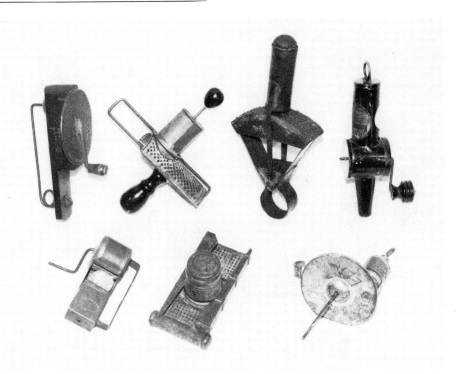

Mechanical nutmeg graters: (*top row*) Common Sense, 1867, **$450–$495**; The Edgar, **$75–$85**; black painted grater, c. 1875, **$525–$595**; The Rapid, brown asphaltum, **$400–$425**; (*bottom row*) grater Pat. Nov. 1855, **$375–$395**; center grater, **$165–$185**; Carsley, Lynn, Massachusetts, **$600–$650**.

Sterling silver nutmeg graters: box grater with storage for nutmegs, **$650–$695**; mechanical grater, **$1200–$1400**; grater that pulls out from base of figure, **$650–$695**; mechanical grater, **$895–$995**.

Milliner's model, **$850–$1000**; courting mirror, **$750–$850**.

Paper bandbox. The bandbox was originally used by men and women to store and carry starched ruffs (the kind we see in old portraits). Ladies used the boxes for bonnets, ribbons, hair pieces, jewelry, and other accessories. The wallpaper pattern on this box is Clayton's Ascent on blue ground. **$950–$1000**

Doris Stauble arrangement, old cherries in blue spongeware bowl. **$325–$375**

Doris Stauble arrangement, wax apples in blue carrier surrounded by old millinery material. **$350–$395**

Framed Shaker labels, herb labels used on jars by the Shaker community in Mount Lebanon, New York. **$450–$495**

Mocha ware: mug with blue seaweed banding, **$375–$395**; pitcher with green seaweed banding, **$375–$395**.

Blue onion canisters: powdered sugar, **$165–$175**; loaf sugar, **$250–$275**; sugar, **$145–$155**.

Blue onion utensils: ladle, **$150–$175**; strainer, **$250–$275**.

Tiered cake stands, **$75–$145** each; stone fruits, **$75–$95** each; stone nuts and berries (not common), **$75–$95** each.

Blown jar with gold scrolled label, most likely used in a general store. **$200–$225**

Wood pigeon decoys: *(left)* **$395–$425**; *(right)* with sculptured tail feathers, **$450–$495**.

Wooden house banks, painted buildings which were popular in the early 1900s for saving coins. **$175–$195**

Papier mâché fish candy containers, colorful, painted, hinged lid on back. **$375–$575**

Bliss dollhouse, lithographed paper covers house. **$495–$595**

German dollhouse, front swings open to reveal room interiors, old lace curtains. **$550–$595**

Wooden rocking horse, leather seat, carved body and rockers. **$1400–$1600**

Miniature folk art horse, copper with verdigris patina. **$650**

Child's horse on platform with wheels, dappled gray paint, iron wheels. A small child could be pulled on this horse. **$1200–$1400**

Gray enamel cream pail, tin lid, wire handle. **$40–$45**

Brass and nickel-plated ice cream scoops. **$80–$110**

Squirrel windmill weight; this is a small example of the weights used on windmills around 1890. **$500–$575**

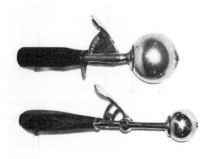

Ice cream scoops: nickel-plated scoop, Bakelite handle, marked "Williamson, Belleville, N.J.," **$35–$40**; sherbet-size scoop, brass stem and lever, nickel-plated, wood handle, **$110–$125**.

123

Hamilton Beach #31 ice cream scoop, formerly Gilchrist #31. **$125–$150**

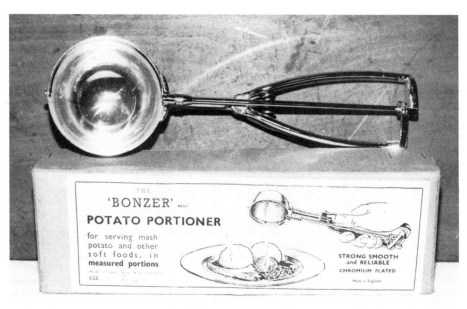

Bronze potato portioner. **$225–$275**

S. S. Hersey apple peeler, patented June 18, 1861, cast iron. **$185–$225**

Apple peeler, marked "Reading Hardware Works, Reading, Pa." on main gear. Patented May 5, 1868. "Manufactured by Harbster Bros." marked on gear mount. **$125–$150**

Peach parer, made by Sinclair Scott Co., Baltimore. **$175–$195**

Stoneware

Rare Union Hill, New Jersey, three-gallon jar with a delicate bird and branch decoration. **$600–$700**

A piece of stoneware is usually evaluated on the basis of its form, maker's mark, decoration, and condition. If a "perfect" three-gallon ovoid jug is found in the basement of an early nineteenth-century home and it carries an incised eagle and a maker's mark, all the criteria for great value have been met. However, the odds of this happening are slim and falling, and in fact most collectors of decorated stoneware would be pleased to discover an E. and L. P. Norton jug (1865–1881) with a brush-executed cobalt bird with a minor crack and a $450 price tag.

As the supply of decorated crocks, churns, and jugs from New York, Pennsylvania, and New England has diminished during the past decade, many collectors have turned to the more affordable and available late nineteenth-century thrown and molded examples from Illinois, Minnesota, and Indiana as an alternative. This shift has brought about a change in the price structure and marketing of a great deal of American stoneware. The market for this later stoneware tends to be much more regional than national. While decorated stoneware with elaborate birds and flowers is as eagerly collected in

Maine and New York as in Iowa and California, White Hall Pottery from Scott County, Illinois, for example, brings enthusiastic bids at local auctions in the Land of Lincoln but not in Idaho or Rhode Island.

With the market and prices for American folk art rising almost daily, it would appear that stoneware decorated with cobalt flowers or birds and having a minimum of cracks, chips, and flakes might not be a bad investment if priced in the $300 to $500 range. The amount of later, regional stoneware is still sufficient to meet local demands for a long time, and pieces of such stoneware in questionable condition should be purchased for a low price, and only after considerable thought.

Decoration Rarity Scale

	Commonly found*	Not commonly found	Rare	Extremely rare
Swirls and geometric designs	X			
Flowers		X		
Birds			X	
Animals			X	
Scenes (ships, houses, trees)			X	
People				X

* Note the following explanations of the rarity designations used:

Commonly found: Can often be found at farm sales, flea markets, antiques malls, and house or tag sales.

Not commonly found: Can be found at some antiques shows and shops, but usually will require some serious effort to locate.

Rare: Occasionally can be found at "important" antiques shows and exceptional shops that specialize in American country antiques for serious collectors; usually takes deep pockets and a significant investment of time to find.

Extremely rare: Handled by less than a dozen dealers in the United States. Examples seldom reach the general market and are usually quickly sold within a small network of dealers and collectors.

Dating Decorated Stoneware

This diagram presents a broad overview of decorative techniques and the time frames in which they were used by American stoneware potteries during the nineteenth and early twentieth centuries.

Types of Decoration	1800	1820	1840	1860	1880	1900–1925
Incised		▓▓▓▓▓				
Brushed			▓▓▓▓▓▓▓▓▓▓			
Slip-trailed			▓▓▓▓▓▓			
Stenciled and brushed				▓▓▓		
Stenciled					▓▓▓▓▓▓▓▓	

Keene, New Hampshire, jug with bird design. **$350–$400**

Ovoid three-gallon jug with brushed flower. **$300–$335**

Three-gallon "bird" jug from Norton Pottery, Worcester, Massachusetts. **$600–$675**

New York Stoneware Co. (Fort Edward) four-gallon jug with cobalt floral spray. **$325–$350**

Two-gallon jug with complex floral spray executed with a slip cup. **$400–$450**

Three-gallon jug with slip-trailed flower. $300–$350

Semi-ovoid four-gallon jug with brushed flower, Lyons, New York. $300–$350

Athens, New York, two-gallon ovoid jug from Clark Pottery with brushed flower design. $325–$375

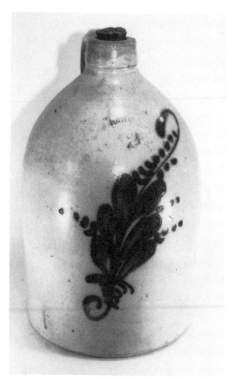

Two-gallon jug with cobalt floral spray.
$275–$325

Three-gallon "bird" jug from Ft. Edward,
New York. **$400–$425**

Three-gallon floral spray jug, Bennington,
Vermont. **$335–$375**

Three-gallon jug with crudely done slip-trailed bird on a branch. **$500–$575**

Three-gallon jug from Whites Pottery of Utica, New York. **$250–$300**

Four-gallon jug with cobalt tulip. **$275–$325**

Three-gallon jug with cobalt floral spray and pouring spout from Ft. Edward, New York. **$300–$375**

Vendor's jug with impressed name and cobalt bird from Poughkeepsie, New York. **$400–$450**

Three-gallon "thrown" vendor's jug from A. McClure and Co. of Albany, New York, **$65–$75**; two-gallon molded "platform" liquor jug from Owensboro, Kentucky, **$65–$75**.

Miniature whiskey jug with incised "Compliments of John Rhodes," Albany slip. **$125–$140**

Noah White and Sons two-gallon slip-trailed jug from Utica, New York. **$300–$375**

One-gallon jug with deep cobalt bird, Binghamton, New York. **$500–$600**

Jug with slip-trailed flowers, J. & E. Norton, Bennington, Vermont. **$400–$450**

Unusual incised two-gallon vendor's jug from Whitehall, New York, with brushed decoration. **$400–$500**

Three-gallon jug with cobalt pot of flowers. **$325–$350**

New York Stoneware Company two-gallon jug with elaborate brushed cobalt bird. **$550–$650**

Five gallon "platform" jug, molded with Albany slip and Bristol glaze. **$45–$55**

Three-gallon ovoid jug from Albany, New York. **$150–$175**

Two-gallon New York State "bird" jug.
$335–$375

Two-gallon jug with cobalt wreath. **$250–$325**

Vendor's jug with brushed label, made by Cooperative Pottery, Lyons, New York. **$125–$150**

138

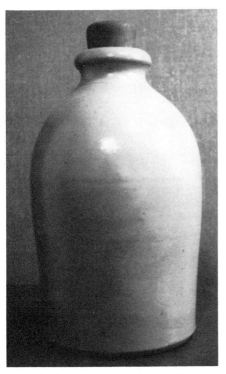

Unmarked and undecorated one-gallon jug, Bristol glaze. **$35–$50**

New York State "bird" jug, two-gallon. **$375–$425**

Two-gallon jug with slip-trailed bird design. **$500–$600**

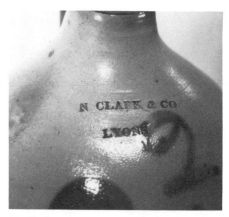

Impressed "4" capacity mark and "New York Stoneware Co. Fort Edward, N.Y." This pottery did business from approximately 1861 to 1891 under the name New York Stoneware Co.

N. Clark and Co., Lyons, New York, 1825–1852.

It is possible to get an approximate date for the operation of a particular pottery by checking the name with a reference source. Webster's *Decorated Stoneware of North America* (Charles E. Tuttle Co.) provides collectors with a wealth of data about the periods of operation.

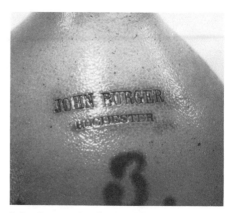

John Burger, Rochester, New York, 1860s.

J. & E. Norton, Bennington, Vermont, 1850–1861.

Between 1839 and 1894 there were various combinations of Nortons and Fentons in the stoneware factory at Bennington, Vermont. The pottery works at Bennington are probably the most documented and researched of all stoneware operations.

L. E. Holdridge is the name of the businessman or vendor who had his name impressed on jugs that were made to hold his product.

Two-gallon unmarked crock depicting chicken pecking corn. **$800–$1000**

Two-gallon Norton crock with slip-trailed floral spray. **$500–$650**

Decorated four-gallon crock with brushed cobalt flower, Lyons, New York. **$450–$525**

Two-gallon crock with slip-trailed bird. **$900–$1200**

Unmarked five-gallon crock with double birds on a branch. **$1200–$1500**

Braun Pottery, Buffalo, New York, six-gallon crock with slip-trailed floral decoration. **$500–$600**

Five-gallon Monmouth, Illinois, crock with stenciled decoration. **$65–$75**

Six-gallon crock, stenciled decoration. **$50–$75**

Crock, S. Hart, Fulton, New York. **$550–$700**

Six-gallon Burger and Company crock, Rochester, New York. **$425–$500**

Crock with deep cobalt bird on a stump, four gallon. **$600–$725**

Four-gallon unmarked crock, cobalt robin. **$450–$550**

Crock, S. Hart, Fulton, New York, two-gallon with slip-trailed dog. **$1500–$1800**

Three-gallon crock with simple slip-trailed swirls. **$100–$135**

Unmarked crock dated "1895"; damage to rim and front dramatically lowers value: **$200–$225** as is, **$375–$425** if perfect.

Unmarked stoneware bottle dipped in blue cobalt. **$50–$60**

Ovoid jar with brushed flower. **$275–$325**

J. & E. Norton 1½-gallon jar with slip-trailed bird. **$600–$700**

Unmarked jar with elaborate slip-trailed bird and leaf in deep cobalt.

Molded stoneware bottles with any kind of decoration or mark are fairly difficult to find. These molded bottles date from the second half of the nineteenth century.

Burger two-gallon jar from Rochester, New York, slip-trailed flower. **$350–$450**

Three-gallon Hamilton and Jones, Greensboro, Pennsylvania, jar with stenciled and brushed decoration. **$500–$575**

Canning jar with stenciled label and brushed decoration at top and bottom, from Louisville, Kentucky. **$175–$225**

Stoneware jar from North Carolina, early nineteenth century. **$250–$300**

Unmarked stoneware fruit jar from the late nineteenth century with world class glaze flaking. **$15–$20**

Simple Pennsylvania redware jar, Albany slip decoration. **$60–$70**

Four-gallon jar from Cortland, New York, with cobalt flowers. **$650–$725**

Athens, New York, four-gallon jar with slip-trailed abstract floral decoration. **$550–$700**

Three-gallon jar with cobalt floral spray from the Norton Pottery, Worcester, Massachusetts. **$550–$650**

Rare Union Hill, New Jersey, three-gallon jar with a delicate bird and branch decoration. **$600–$700**

Rare five-gallon Fort Edward, New York, stoneware jar with elaborate bird and floral spray. **$750–$1000**

Two-gallon New York State jar with slip-trailed cobalt flower. **$375–$425**

Decorated stoneware batter jar with bale handle and pouring spout, probably from Pennsylvania. **$850–$1000**

Two-gallon stoneware jar from the Hart Pottery decorated with bird on a flower stem. **$550–$750**

Four-gallon churn with floral spray decoration, Ottman Bros., Fort Edward, New York. **$1000–$1200**

Pennsylvania churn with stenciled eagle. **$900–$1200**

Two-gallon Monmouth, Illinois, stoneware churn with stenciled decoration. **$175–$225**

Stoneware pitcher, unmarked, Albany slip. **$100–$125**

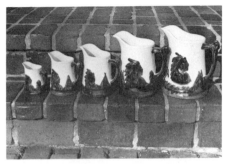

Set of five Sleepy Eye pitchers from the Monmouth Pottery. **$1500–$1800** set

Reverse side of the Lincoln pitcher showing the log cabin in which Lincoln was born.

Molded Abe Lincoln pitcher, White Hall Pottery, White Hall, Illinois. **$300–$350**

Molded stoneware pitcher from the early twentieth century. **$50–$60**

Rockingham pitcher, commonly referred to as Bennington-type, late nineteenth century. **$225–$275**

Molded stoneware pitcher with embossed decoration. **$150–$175**

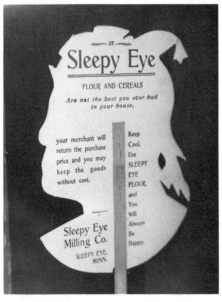

Redware pitcher and milk pan from Pennsylvania, unmarked, mid-nineteenth century: pitcher, **$200–$225**; milk pan, **$300–$375**.

"Rebecca at the Well" molded pitcher, c. 1880. **$200–$225**

Sleepy Eye promotional fan. **$200–$225**

Sleepy Eye sugar and creamer. **$400–$500** set

Sleepy Eye stein. **$400–$500**

Sleepy Eye mugs. **$200–$225** each

Sleepy Eye vase. **$500–$575**

Molded spongeware butter crock. **$200–$250**

Sleepy Eye steins. **$400–$600** each

Molded stoneware rolling pins given as premiums, maple handles. **$150–$175** each

Transfer-decorated coffee and tea set, molded. **$150** set

Molded Wesson Oil jar, stenciled label. $150–$175

Stoneware salt crock, "as found" condition, stenciled decoration. $50–$65

Molded stoneware sugar bowl. $125–$150

Molded stoneware butter crock, stenciled label, Bristol glaze. $100–$125

Rare stoneware canteen, embossed decoration, from New York State. **$200–$275**

Molded spongeware mixing bowl. **$125–$150**

Molded stoneware spongeware bowl. **$125–$150**

Spongeware bowls. **$125–$150** each

Stoneware salt crock with replaced wooden lid, **$50–$100**; "6¢" stoneware bowl, **$50–$75**.

Molded yelloware bowl. **$45–$60**

Sponge-decorated bowl. **$125–$150**

Country Antiques Shops and Malls

Carved wood rooster, traces of old red, blue, and gold paint, 16″ tall. **$350**

One of the most significant changes over the past decade for collectors of country antiques is the opportunity to make purchases within an hour's drive of most communities in the United States. This was not the case in the 1970s.

Collecting Americana is no longer limited by geography. There are as many serious collectors in California and Oregon as in Ohio and Pennsylvania, and shops, markets, and malls have been opened to meet the growing demand for quality items.

In this chapter we have included pictures and prices of country antiques in California and in Kentucky to provide a national perspective on price trends.

Creekside Antiques

Twenty minutes north of San Francisco is the small community of San Anselmo. San Anselmo offers visitors more than 120 dealers offering a wide variety of antiques.

Creekside Antiques, is a collective shop with 15 dealers who specialize in early Americana, country, and folk art. The inventory ranges from early textiles, folk art, pottery, clocks, and toys, to early lighting and American furniture.

Folk art is a very popular and compelling draw in California, and there are many collectors interested in wood figural carvings, paintings, whirligigs, weather vanes, tavern signs, samplers, and hooked and braided rugs.

Creekside Antiques was the inspiration of Pat Newsom, who began the business in July of 1988. Creekside Antiques may be contacted at the address below:

Creekside Antiques
241 Sir Francis Drake
San Anselmo, California 94960
(415) 457-1266

Pair of oil paintings, artist unknown, c. 1830. **$2800** pair

Maple chest of drawers, 1830s. **$650**

Victorian natural wicker rocker and floor lamp, 1920s: lamp, **$700**; rocker, **$800**.

Old rabbit jalopy, 1940s, **$325**; Bing tractor, **$495**.

Stick box with "Anna" inlaid. **$450**

Cherry Sheraton chest of drawers with her-ringbone inlay, c. 1810. **$2200**

Splay-legged cherry nightstand, 1840s. **$595**

American tole tray, c. 1820. **$1100**

Primitive painting of horses, Kentucky. **$850**

Wooden ship model, c. 1910. **$125**

Left to right: Kestner #169, closed mouth, **$1695**; Armand Marseille #985, **$600**.

Cherry blanket chest, signed on back "Col. Cooley USA," found in Virginia, c. 1850, **$1200**; miniature blanket chest, pine, **$650**.

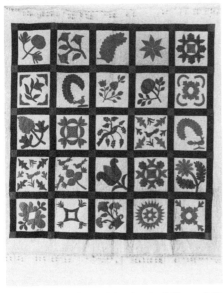

Album quilt from Maryland, 86″ × 86″, c. 1850. **$7500**

Youth chair, early nineteenth century. **$325**

Rocking horse, original condition, early nineteenth century. **$1800**

Hand-wrought iron broiler, eighteenth century. **$375**

Birdhouse from Maine, first quarter of the twentieth century. **$950**

Nineteenth-century carved wood eagle. **$800**

Grain-painted arrowback Windsor settee from Pennsylvania, 1840s. **$2900**

Carved wood rooster, traces of old red, blue, and gold paint, 16″ tall. **$350**

Ventriloquist's doll, hand-carved wooden head, glass eyes, original dress, 4½′ tall. **$1200**

Red-and-white American eagle quilt from Pennsylvania, 80″ × 68″, c. 1920. **$1400**

Eighteenth-century pine blanket chest, lift top. **$800**

Oak apothecary chest. **$1200**

Pine step-back cupboard, mid-nineteenth century. **$2200**

Step-back pine cupboard, c. 1840. **$2500**

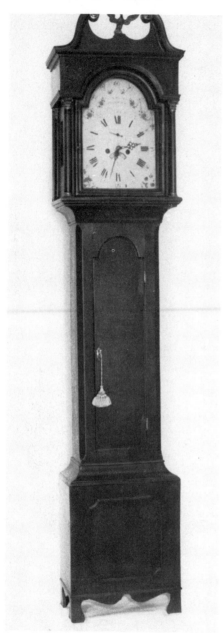

Wooden stick figure with composition head, 11" tall. **$250**

Eight-day walnut long-case clock, John Smith, Burwick, Maine. **$6900**

Tilt-top candlestand, mahogany with maple inlay, snake feet, c. 1840. **$1300**

Folky five-drawer miniature dresser. **$245**

United States Air Force quilt. **$1800**

Painted tin shield, c. 1910. **$650**

Sawbuck table, pine, 1820s. **$2500**

Lancaster Antique Market

The Lancaster Antique Market is located near Shakertown at Pleasant Hill. The mall contains more than 20,000 square feet of Americana and is open daily from 10 a.m. to 5 p.m. Monday through Saturday and from 1 p.m. to 5 p.m. on Sunday. For a fee of $10, the Lancaster Antique Market offers a narrated videotape of items that currently are for sale (the fee is refundable with purchase). Antiques are shipped daily by United Parcel Service (UPS) and by freight.

Lancaster Antique Market
102 Hamilton Avenue
Lancaster, Kentucky 40444
(606) 792-4536

Pair of 1920s iron candle holders. **$95**

Miniature gray graniteware: coffeepot, **$75**; kettle, **$95**; trivet, **$65**.

Drying tray of splint. **$250**

Pennsylvania Sheraton walnut chest of drawers with quarter-moon inlay. **$3000**

Walnut 12-pane step-back cupboard in early finish, Kentucky. **$2800**

A 1930s doll dressed by the Shakers for sale in their community gift shops. **$895**

One-drawer stand found in New Hampshire, **$295**; two-drawer decorated box, **$125**.

One of a pair of black step-down Windsor chairs. **$695** pair

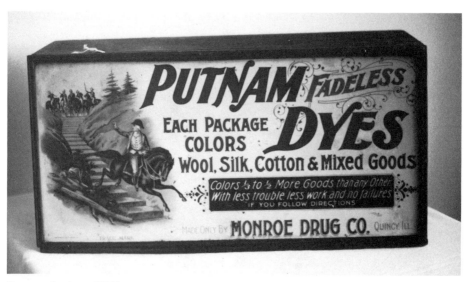

Putnam dye box. **$150**

Iron doorstop, basket of flowers with original painted finish. **$95**

Lapped bucket in mustard paint. **$250**

Pennsylvania grain-painted pine chimney cupboard, c. 1880. **$1250**

Unusual basket form with wooden runners in brown paint. **$295**

Twelve-tin pie safe in green paint. **$800**

Walnut crock cupboard, Kentucky. **$850**

Miniature cupboard. **$250**

Shaker table in gray paint, Union Village, Ohio. **$1250**

Large cast iron shooting gallery target, traces of old paint, 22″ wing span. **$350**

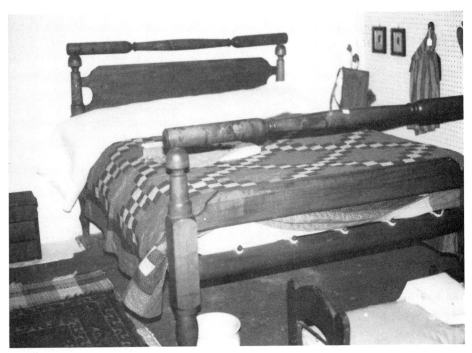

Curly maple rope bed, c. 1870. **$395**

Antiquing Across the Midwest

Gary and Susan Sheets reside in Normal, Illinois, with their two children.

If your heart beats fast at the sight of a painted cupboard or an old quilt worn from many years of use, or if you have knots in your stomach at the sight of an "Antiques Ahead" sign while the kids in the back seat groan in agony, it's safe to say you've been bitten by the antiques bug.

Our quest for antiques started 10 years ago when we stumbled upon a Bullard & Scott "bird" crock for $20. Since then we have been hooked. Unfortunately, you cannot find "bird" crocks for $20 anymore, but you can still unearth a few treasures if you look in the right places.

The Midwestern states of Illinois, Iowa, and Indiana are well known for their abundance of golden-oak furniture and Depression glass. If this is your idea of a dream come true, then central Illinois and Indiana are your gold mine. If you prefer the more primitive furniture, you have to search a little harder, but it's still out there.

The Midwest is also famous for farm estate auctions. Occasionally amid all the farm implements and plywood television stands you can find a wonderful collection of old baskets or firkins that somebody's grandmother put in the attic 50 years ago. There is a word of caution, though. Prices at auctions can be extremely high or very low, depending upon whom you are bidding against. You can almost guarantee that an auction that has been highly advertised in an antiques paper or magazine will attract many dealers and serious collectors who are willing to pay premium prices. Just be sure that you have

a levelheaded bidder on your side, or else check your emotions at the door. If you don't, you could end up paying three times as much for something as your common sense or pocketbook would have otherwise allowed.

Another option for weekend antiquing is piling the kids in the back of the Volvo and hitting all the open-air markets and one-day antiques shows. There are some very good bargains to be found if you head out early enough with a copy of *Antique Week* (Knightstown, Indiana) and a road atlas.

Some shows allow "early bird" buying which allows you to look for a few hours before the general public is admitted. There is always a fee, but if you're serious about the hunt, it's well worth the extra money for the head start. By the end of the day you may have a cache of wonderful finds or a migraine from the combination of your children and your inability to find anything.

For those of us that have to be on the hunt 365 days a year there is always the trip to the local or area antiques mall. Antiques malls usually have a variety of merchandise from contemporary and Victorian to country. While there are some very good malls with high-quality items, there are also some that offer merchandise that resembles the 10¢ table at a garage sale.

Over the years we have watched prices go up as fast as our children are growing up. People who laughed at us spending $20 on a hog scrapper candlestick years ago are now standing in line to pay $150 for one today. In our fast-paced, mass-produced society, people are learning to appreciate all the time, effort, and craftsmanship that went into making that old cupboard or dry sink a great piece of country furniture.

Some people say that country is "dead," but we believe that there will always be a yearning for the simplicity that country antiques represent and that nothing can replace the thrill of finding a special piece you have been hunting for.

Advertising and Country Store Collectibles

Happy Bunny egg dye: each package, **$4.50**; display box, **$8**

We are convinced that almost everything ever commercially produced by a company or by someone in the United States is collected somewhere by somebody. Those somebodies know the variations in packaging, dates of manufacture, and relative values of whatever it is that they cannot live without. The search may be a lifelong pursuit or only a momentary hobby, but it usually becomes of paramount importance for the duration of the obsession.

It doesn't make any difference if the hunt is centered on Windsor chairs or peanut butter jars. For those of us who collect, the amount of elation can be the same whenever we find one that we don't have at a price we can pay. For many of us the hunt itself is the primary joy of collecting, and the anticipation of finding the item is usually more satisfying than the actual discovery.

Old Storefront Antiques

The Old Storefront Antiques specializes in country store items, pharmaceutical antiques, and collectible advertising. The Old Storefront offers 18 general catalogs of merchandise for sale by mail. The catalogs are $1.50 each or $25 for all 18. A listing of the catalogs according to subject (tins, soda fountain, pharmaceutical, etc.) is available by sending a self-addressed stamped envelope to:

Patricia McDaniel
Old Storefront Antiques
Post Office Box 357
Dublin, Indiana 47335
(317) 478-4809

Wooden box end and small bottle used for Pluto concentrated spring water: box end, **$27**; small bottle, **$17**.

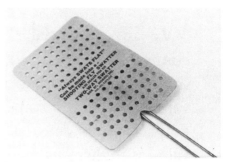

Flyswatter, "Always SWATS FLAT." **$12**

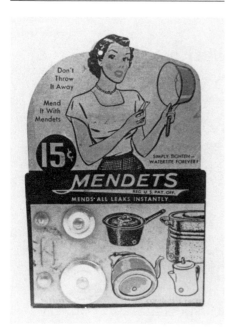

Mendets (mends graniteware). **$10**

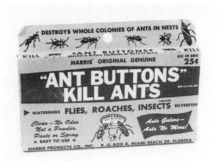

"Ant Buttons" (kills ants). **$7**

Knorpp's birthday cake candle holders (1914). **$18**

Morton Salt display. **$160**

Sellers kitchen cabinet cooking chart. **$50**

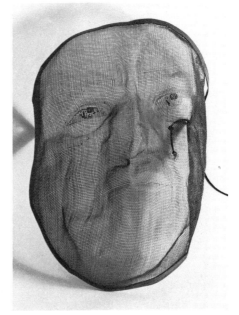

Loyal Order of the Red Men mesh mask. **$150**

Electrocuter electric mousetraps. **$15** each

Health Club baking powder grocer's "Want Book." **$14**

Happy Bunny egg dye: each package, **$4.50**; display box, **$8**

Wooden turnip kraut cutter. **$150**

Girl clothes hanger made of heavy cardboard. **$150**

Baby Ruth chewing gum. **$12**

Dr LeGear's stock powder. **$15**

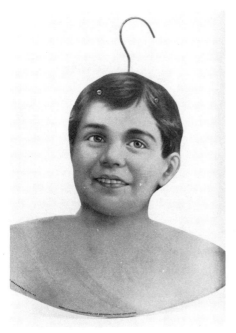

Boy clothes hanger made of heavy cardboard. **$150**

Doom bug killer. **$22**

$1000 Guaranteed bedbug killer. **$10**

Blue Ribbon baking powder (in Ball canning jar, Muncie, Indiana). **$20**

Topsy whitewash brush, "Set in Bakelite." **$10**

Aer-Aid, "Absorbs Refrigerator Odors." **$16**

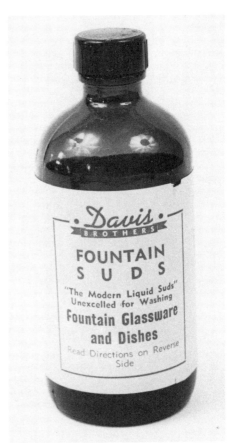

Davis Brothers Fountain Suds. **$12**

Rub-No-More cleanser. **$30**

Epsom salts tin. **$125**

Butterfly Tints. **$7**

Yourex Silver Saver. **$55**

Klex pumice soap. **$7**

Octagon white toilet soap. **$5.50**

Heinz tomato ketchup store display bottle (was always empty). **$55**

Ethyl cleaner, concentrated. **$8.50**

Berko Vigortone. **$6.50**

Thayer and Chandler Hibbard's Roman Gold. **$14**

Fine Feathers Hosiery advertisement. **$15**

Preserve jar labels. **$8.50**

La Dore's Bust Food. **$50**

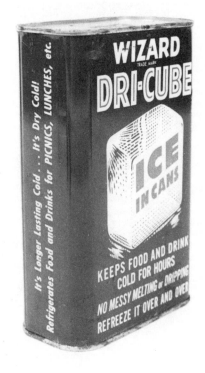

Wilknit hosiery samples. **$17**

Wizard Dri-Cube (dry ice). **$7.50**

Wampole's Preparation. **$8.50**

"Super Market Coloring Contest" book (advertises name brand products). **$18**

Wooden Johnson & Johnson display (Red Cross). **$70**

Snow Crop advertising bear. **$200**

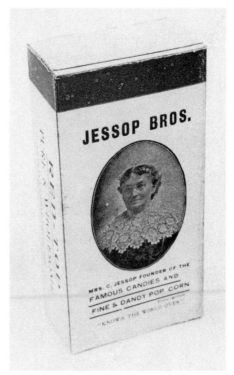

Jessop Bros. popcorn box. **$10**

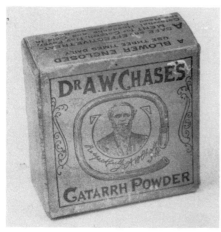

Dr. A. W. Chase's catarrh powder. **$10**

Box from Snow Crop Quick Frozen Waffles. **$17**

Hamburg Breast Tea. **$20**

Great Seal ammonia bottle. **$16**

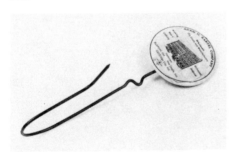

Adam H. Bartel bill hook. **$55**

R and R Carbolized Mutton Tallow tin, free sample. **$8.50**

Spurlock's Southern Laundry Washing Blue. **$15**

Virgin olive oil tin. **$60**

Mallard prepared mustard jar. **$25**

Fownes Gloves: gloves, **$12**; glove measure, **$15**.

Ladies high-top shoes, brown and black. **$135**

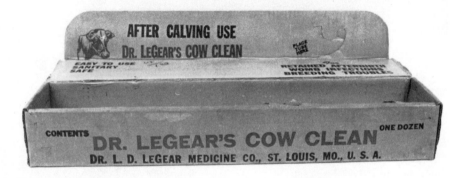

Dr. LeGear's Cow Clean: each tube, **$15**; extra sets of instructions, **$3.50**; display box, **$17**.

Medical assortment, 666 brand: cold tablets (12 tablets), **$7**; cold preparation with quinine (4. oz.), **$8.50**; cold preparation (6 oz.), **$10**; cold capsules (36 tablets), **$9.50**.

WB/W teaspoons (3 dozen). **$45**

Smith Brothers' cough syrup. **$15**

Hansdown hand cleaner. **$10**

666 display box. **$145**

666 display box plus items.

Moore's sheet soap book. **$26**

Renner floating coffee cooker. **$19**

Quaker Oats crayons. **$18**

Purity sheet soap book. **$26**

Papier mâché milk bottle, "Order a Quart of Delicious Chocolate Flavored Milk" (store display). **$30**

Christmas cigarette house, Camel. **$15**

Christmas cigarette house, Salem. **$13**

Domes of Silence (casters). **$12**

Sergeant's Skip-Stain (used to prevent pet stains). **$8**

George F. Cram marking pencils. **$7**

Cardinal Meteor flints and wicks. **$16**

Canada Dry quinine water. **$12**

Chi-namel furniture polish. **$15**

High and Dry soap holder. **$6**

Empress Hosiery box. **$11**

Putnam's Bath Bloom display box (4 packages). **$10**

Putnam's Bath Bloom, package only. **$2.50**

Wright's liquid smoke. **$12**

Innerclean Herbal Laxative. **$7**

Chinaman laundry bag. **$45**

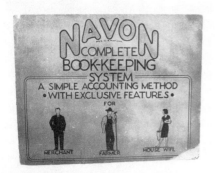

Navon Complete Book-keeping System. **$15**

Germania herb tea. **$8.50**

Gem City Ice Cream sign (chocolate marshmallow). **$45**

St. Joseph Aspirin clock. **$130**

Fru-Tola dispenser. **$375**

Baker's glass store jar. **$85**

National Biscuit Company wood and glass display case. **$375**

Dustdown tin. **$95**

Maroc baby powder tin. **$20**

"Frogletts" tin (Durante's Cough Tablets): "A Froglett a Day Keeps Your Cough Away." **$160**

Cupid Chaser. **$21**

Regoes rubbed sage tin. **$18**

Syrup of Figs and Elixir of Senna (California Fig Syrup Co.), free sample. **$35**

Seaco tin thread holder. **$68**

Cardboard advertising display for Spry shortening. **$80**

Wooden milk box, "Return to Walker Gordon." **$130**

Nordmann's Original canned pumpernickel bread tin. **$12**

Duck Bones tin. **$85**

Bean-X (strings green beans), c. WW II. **$22**

Jar of crushed peach, The Cincinnati Extract Works. **$50**

Breakstone's Pop Corn Style creamed cottage cheese tin. **$40**

Hoosier Club coffee tin. **$165**

Purina Dog Chow sample. **$16**

Quaker Oats price marker. **$12**

Dunn's Coffee Shops cup and plate. **$40**

Mazola corn popper. **$65**

Doan pedal pads. **$8**

Assortment of Saraka tins: trial size, **$35**; 10 oz., **$22**; 1½ lb., **$27**

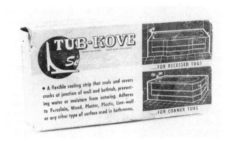

Tub-Kove sealing strip. **$12**

Private Shops and Collections

The advertising items and country store collectibles that follow were taken from private collections, antiques shops, shows, and malls.

Candy tin from Bloomington, Illinois, made to resemble a workman's lunch pail, c. 1930. **$75–$85**

Grape-Nuts tin from the first quarter of the twentieth century. **$50–$60**

None-Such peanut butter pail. **$50–$55**

Tin Putnam dye cabinet. **$65–$75**

Sample size Happy Hour coffee tin. **$15–$20**

Display container with removable label for Cough Cherries. **$100–$125**

Lucky Strike metal container, c. 1915. **$15–$20**

Rawleigh's cinnamon container. **$10–$15**

Calumet baking powder tin. $5–$7

Lemon wafer tin. $8–$12

Old Judge coffee container. $20–$25

Old Label baking powder container. $10–$12

"Hand Made" tobacco tin. **$12–$15**

Peter Hauptmann's Mixture (tobacco) tin. **$10–$12**

Granger pipe tobacco container. **$20–$25**

Sir Walter Raleigh smoking tobacco container. **$8–$12**

Burnham Bartlett pears tin can. **$7–$9**

Edgeworth tobacco tin (pocket). **$8–$10**

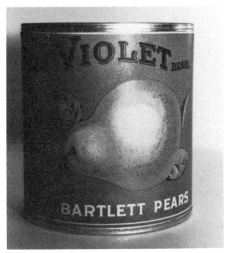

Violet Bartlett pears. **$7–$9**

Krak-R-Jak Biscuits container. **$20–$24**

211

Jolly Time Pop Corn tin. **$12–$15**

Sahadi's Halwah circular tin. **$12–$15**

Queen's Taste coffee tin. **$15–$20**

Ezra Williams flower seeds box. **$300–$350**

Mason's shoe polish box with paper labels. **$100–$135**

Coca-Cola tray, early 1920s. **$200–$225**

Stickney & Poor's Mustard box. **$225–$250**

Shakers' Garden Seeds box (without lid). **$500–$600**

Neck of Land order box from Virginia brewery. **$350–$400**

Hart's Seeds jars, 1950s. **$10–$15**

Glass seed jars from country store. **$20–$25** each

J. & P. Coats display case with pullout shelves. **$150–$200**

Star Threads oak display cabinet. **$350–$450**

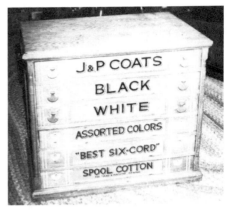

J. & P. Coats spool chest, oak. **$400–$475**

Coffee grinder from grocery store, made by Elgin, original painted finish. **$300–$400**

J. & P. Coats spool chest, oak. **$300–$375**

Chicago American newspaper street corner vendor's box. **$375–$450**

Counter display container for the Boye Needle Company. **$200–$250**

F. F. Schmalz & Sons cash register, early 1900s. **$200–$300**

Brass stencil for Jersey Sweet Potatoes containers. **$30–$35**

Sign from government building indicating days closed due to "legal holidays," c. 1915. **$65–$85**

"The City Candy Kitchen" tin sign, hand-lettered, framed in pine, from shop in Wisconsin, 1920s. **$275–$350**

Lantern made into an "Ice Cream and Pop" sign, from an Ohio general store, c. 1900. **$225–$250**

Tom's Toasted Peanuts counter jar, c. 1950. **$50–$75**

Oak case and counter section from rural Illinois post office, c. 1920. **$400–$475**

Collection of wooden boxes with paper labels.

Dan Patch Cut Plug tin. **$40–$50**

Collecting
Duck Decoys

This section was prepared by John and Mary Purvis, nationally known dealers of antique duck decoys. They participate in shows throughout the United States, selling to dealers, collectors, and novices. They maintain a mail-order business out of their home at 50609 Bellfort Court, New Baltimore, Michigan 48047, (313) 725-2179.

Mallard drake, Wildfowler Decoy Company. Near mint original paint, Balsa body, **$200–$300**. If the decoy had the company stamp, it could go for a much higher price.

No one would buy a new car with a crunched fender and a repainted hood. However, a 1957 Chevrolet with those problems would be a different matter. The same concept is true for decoys. A brand-new decoy should be all new, all original, while a classic decoy that is 40, 50, or 100 years old is certainly acceptable in a less-than-perfect condition.

Historical Perspective

A hunter goes out to the marsh. He takes his decoys. Some he has bought, some he has made, and the rest are "hand me downs" from an older brother, his father, or his grandfather. Casually he tosses the decoys out into the water as generations before him have done. He fires his gun over and sometimes into the decoys. At the end of the day he is cold, wet, tired, and probably mad, and he retrieves his decoys; wraps the anchor line around them; tosses them into the bottom of the boat covered with gas, oil, water, and crumbs from his lunch; and heads for shore. He then piles the decoys in a shed where they will freeze, thaw, and dry until the next hunting season. During the warm months the hunter repairs and repaints his decoys in his own style using materials that are different from those his predecessors used.

If the hunter's son is a conservationist he will save several of his father's decoys and sell the rest. What are the decoys worth? They are obviously worth much more than the grandfather and father originally paid for them. The paint may be old, rotten, or gone, and there are cracks, tears, chips, and dry rot; but they have original form, honest age, and historical significance, and they are true American folk art. They have value for all these reasons.

The value is determined by many things. We would like to explore some of the terminology of decoy collecting with an emphasis on how values are affected by various factors that relate to the terminology. We also present some general terms that may add to the enjoyment of decoys.

Valuation Criteria

Carver

Who made the decoy—a factory or an individual carver? There are some big names among the carvers. A small sampling would include Joe Lincoln, Ira Hudson, Elmer Crowell, Ben Schmidt, Lem Dudley, and the Ward brothers. The factory names of Mason, Dodge, Animal Trap, Wildfowler, Evans, and Pratt are also important. Such major names add a great deal to the value of a decoy.

Age

Generally, for decoys as for other antiques age is an advantage.

Many carvers worked for a long time and created hundreds of decoys. Several of the carvers were active in the 1940s, 1950s, and 1960s, and a few are still carving decoys today. Some of the later works of the better known carvers are as valuable as their earlier efforts.

Most decoys collected today date from about 1925 to 1950. Our own collection contains decoys that were made between the 1870s and 1950. It is often difficult to prove the age of a decoy. The date of the carver's death can be used as a basic time frame, as can the initials of the hunter (owner) that might be on the bottom of a decoy. If the provenance of a decoy is available and the original owner can be determined, a great deal of knowledge about the period of use can be obtained.

Paint and Condition

Original paint is paint that was applied to the decoy by the carver. *Working paint,* or *overpaint,* was put on top of the original paint while the decoy was in use.

Form

This seems to be of growing importance to many collectors. It could be called "eye appeal." Even the crudest of decoys attracted ducks and geese; however, some carvers made more realistic decoys that tend to be more accurate and less folky in appearance.

Repairs

Decoys were often damaged in use. Most repairs were done by the hunter. Such repairs include fixing broken bills and cracked necks, filling shot marks, and repainting. In our opinion these repairs detract from value, but they also can add to the history of a decoy if they were done by the hunter.

"Professionally restored" or "professionally repainted" are terms used more frequently recently in auction catalogs. The terms mean that someone has repaired the decoy in hopes of increasing its value. Some values are enhanced by this process, while others are diminished.

Attributions

This is another kind of auction hype. Often merely the carver whom the seller *wishes* had done the work is given credit for a piece. On other occasions the decoy is attributed to a carver sincerely believed to have made the decoy, even though no verification is available.

Eyes

All sorts of eyes were used over the years in the construction of duck decoys. Glass of varying size and quality was a first choice, with tacks and shoe buttons also utilized. Some carvers painted on the eyes.

Bill Carving

One of the little details that often enhances decoy value is the quality of carving performed on the bill. Sometimes a "nail" or "eyetooth" was carved at the end of the bill.

Wing Carving

The delineation of the wings on the back of the decoy is an important feature to examine when evaluating a decoy. Few very early decoys had this carved feature. Most wings were simply delineated by paint rather than by actual carving.

Neck Putty

Commonly used in reference to Mason Standard Grade factory decoys, neck putty was used to enhance the fit of the head and neck joint. Absence of the neck putty can reduce the value of a Mason Standard Grade decoy. Replaced putty can also be a negative factor in the evaluation of a decoy. Most of the time the orignal putty has shrunk and fallen out.

Hollow

Many decoys from the Lake St. Clair and southwestern Ontario areas were carved hollow to reduce the carrying weight of the giant rigs used in those areas. Some decoys were hollowed to a thin shell with a bottom board attached to complete watertightness. Certain factory decoys had a hole drilled from the front through the body which was then plugged before painting. Hollowness can and often does increase a decoy's value.

Scratch Painting

Scratch painting, also called comb painting, was done on the backs of decoys. The carver would use a tool like a comb to cut through a layer of overpaint. This let the color of a lower layer of paint show through, creating a pattern effect that simulated feathering.

Roothead

Decoy heads were sometimes fashioned from the actual roots of trees and shrubs. Pieces of root were chosen to resemble the species. This was quite common in shorebird decoys. A major advantage was the near indestructibility of the head.

Terms

There are a multitude of terms that we could list here. Some of the terms vary around the country. Most of the terms that follow are hunting terms which a collector should be familiar with, if only to better converse about decoys.

Decoy A piece of sculpture made by hand or machine that was used to entice wildfowl into the range of the hunter's weapon.

Stickup A decoy, usually a silhouette, used on land or in shallow water and raised and stabilized by one or more sticks.

Sleeper A decoy with the head turned and the bill lying on the back or seemingly tucked under a wing.

Lowhead A decoy with a very short or nonexistent neck.

Turnhead A decoy looking in a direction other than forward.

Preener A decoy that simulates a duck preening its feathers.

Feeder A decoy that usually shows only body and tail, giving the appearance of a bird eating off the bottom. Feeders are weighted to remain in this eating position. Often feeders are factory-made. Occasionally a feeder decoy is called a "tip-up."

Blind A place of concealment within which the waterfowl hunter hides until the quarry is in range. A blind can be on land or water and is usually formed of native materials.

Flyway One of the major paths waterfowl travel during the spring and fall migrations. The Atlantic, Mississippi, Central, and Pacific are the four flyways in the United States.

Besides those presented here, there are many other terms that are used in conjunction with decoys and hunting. Part of the fun of collecting is learning new terms. There are plenty of books on the subject of decoys. Take advantage of them and also seek out the knowledgable people around the country who love to talk about collecting old decoys.

Pintail drake carved by a member of the Reeves family (probably Charles), Port Rowan, Ontario, c. 1920. Old paint may be part original. Solid body. **$600–$900**

Mallard drake made by Dodge Decoy Factory, Detroit, Michigan (1884–1894). This 100-year-old beauty is a collector's dream. It was never in the water, was never rigged for use, and has near mint original paint with a wonderful patina of age from years of display. **$2000–$3000**

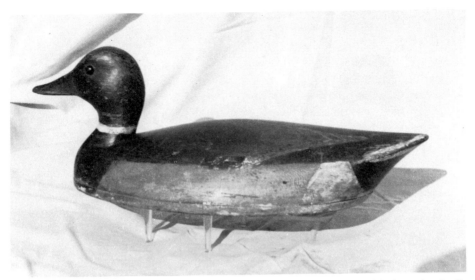

Mallard drake carved by John R. Wells, Toronto, Ontario, early 1900s. This decoy has it all: original paint, hollow, maker's stamp on bottom, made for a future king of England when he came to Manitoba, Canada, to hunt. **$3000–$4000**

Bluebill hen carved by Capt. John Schweikart, Detroit, Michigan (1870–1954). Beautifully carved, hollow, possibly repainted by the carver, oversize of the species. **$800–$900**

Brant carved of redwood by George Kryle of Eureka, California. Very folky, much of the paint may be a stain, slight bill damage, early 1900s. **$400–$500**

Pair of Bluebills by Mason Decoy Factory, Detroit, Michigan (1894–1924). Both are standard grade glass-eye models with working paint. Neck putty replaced in both. Some physical damage visable in front decoy, **$100–$200** each. If original paint and good condition, $300 each.

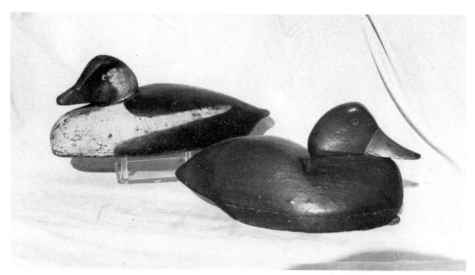

Two small, hollow, lowhead decoys from Lake St. Clair. Front decoy especially folky. Both in old working paint, c. 1900. (*Rear*) Bufflehead, **$600–$900**; (*front*) Redhead, **$500–$600**.

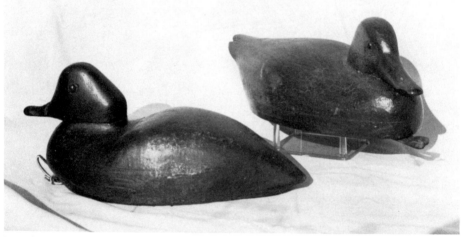

Two hollow lowheads. (*Front*) Lowhead carved by Tom Chambers, Toronto, Ontario, early 1900s; has very old in-use paint, slight chips to bill and tail. If perfect, **$3000–$5000**; as is, **$1200–$1500**. (*Rear*) Unknown carver, Lake St. Clair, Redhead drake, **$500–$600**.

Black duck (oversize) by Herter's, Waseca, Minnesota. Decoy is printed canvas over cork body with pine head and metal band around the bottom. Fairly rare in good condition, **$150–$200**. *Beware*: Herter's went out of business in the 1960s. Decoys made after the company reopened with new owners will not have the value of the old ones do but may look very similar.

Black duck carved by Frank Schmidt, Detroit, Michigan (1879–1960). His more famous brother was Ben Schmidt. Original paint, wing carving, feather stamping, **$300–$400**. (Ben's carving would be $700–$900.)

Black duck carved by David Simandl of Chatham, Ontario, and Caro, Michigan (1926–1973). Beautiful decorative decoy in original paint, **$500–$700**. Simandl often carved in unusual head positions, which are more valuable.

Mallard drake, Wildfowler Decoy Company. Near mint original paint, Balsa body, **$200–$300**. If the decoy had the company stamp, it could go for a much higher price.

Merganser drake carved by John Paxton, Currituck, North Carolina. Metal crest. *Beware*: This is a well-carved, folky piece, fun to look at and enjoyable to own; but it is *new*, made to look old. If authentic, the decoy would probably sell for $15,000–$20,000; as is, **$150–$300**.

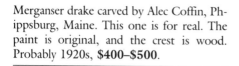

Merganser drake carved by Alec Coffin, Phippsburg, Maine. This one is for real. The paint is original, and the crest is wood. Probably 1920s, **$400–$500**.

Pair Canvasbacks by unknown carver, probably from Wisconsin. Very folky, paint original. A pair can increase the total value, **$250–$350** pair.

Cast iron battery decoy (Redhead drake) from North Carolina. This example is in better condition than most. These are being reproduced today, so be careful. This piece has original paint and limited rust; value is **$400–$500** plus.

Pair Bluebills by Oliver King, Port Severn, Ontario (way up near Georgian Bay, northern Lake Huron). Original paint, very folky, carved and painted eyes; **$200** plus for the pair.

Canvasback drake from Chesapeake Bay, Maryland. The head and body are by different carvers. Replaced heads are not uncommon in that area. Old working paint. **$300–$400**

Coot. The front decoy is by an unknown carver and has old working paint, much cracking and checking, and damaged neck joint; but Coot decoys are rare, **$100**. Rear decoy is by a known carver, Capt. Jessie Urie, Rock Hall, Maryland; thus even though it has been repainted and banged up, the value is greater, **$200–$250**.

Redhead drake carved by Linwood Dudley, Knotts Island, North Carolina (son of very famous carver Lem Dudley). North Carolina decoys tend to be very basic, more folky than beautiful. This decoy is repainted. **$300–$500**

Bluebill drake by Paul Fraley, New Baltimore, Michigan. Solid body, original paint, very stylish, **$75–$100** (most of his decoys are worth less).

Canvasback hen, maker unknown, probably from Quebec. Body is made in several layers (hollowed) with fairly detailed wing carving. With maker unknown, the value is **$50–$75**. If we discover the carver, the value will probably at least double.

Canvasback hen by Budgeon Sampier, Pearl Beach, Michigan. Very old, c. 1900. Hollow with classic Lake St. Clair head, but repainted with a coat of varnish which does detract from value. As is, **$200**; if perfect, much more.

Rare Bufflehead drake by John Way, Prince Edward County, Ontario. Original paint with slight wear, very tiny, **$500–$700**. (*Rear*) Bluebill hen, unknown Ontario carver, mostly original paint, tack-eye, very hollow, **$300–$400.**

Classic Canvasback drake by Art Wilkinson, Leomington, Ontario. Hollow but has poor overpaint on back and sides. **$200–$300**

Canvasback drake, probably by Walter Strubing, Marine City, Michigan. Shows the stipple paint common to that area. Extra value for its very unique swing keel (pivots). **$200–$300**

Canvasback pair carved by Duncan Smith, Chatham, Ontario. The real value of these is that the carver was a shooting partner of Fred Dolsen who is quite famous (his carvings are expensive). These examples from Smith's only rig, c. 1940, all original. **$600–$700** pair

Canvasback drake by unknown carver. Typical of bobtail style used at the Lower Detroit River–Western Lake Erie to reduce buildup of ice and to let the anchor cord slip easily over the back. **$100–$150**.

Canvasback drake by Craig Eitner, New Baltimore, Michigan. Not real old. Would be worth more if not spray-painted, but has classic lines; hollow. **$50–$75**

Canvasaback drake. Very early style by Ed "One-arm" Kellie, Monroe, Michigan. Another bobtail but wider body. Repainted with some damage. The name counts. **$200–$300**

(*Front*) Canvasback drake copying work of Tobin Meldrum. Original Meldrum worth $700–$900. This copy worth **$100**. (*Rear*) Redhead drake, maker unknown. Good paint, very unique keel, bobtail. **$125–$150**

Canvasback drake. Yet another bobtail style from Lake Erie. Remember that each carver had his own theory of how a duck looked on the water and how a decoy would attract. Classic lines, paint may be original. **$100–$150**

Bluebill pair by H. H. Ackerman, Trenton, Michigan. Drake is standard, hen is in resting position. He made *lots* of decoys, generally crude (but they worked), with solid bodies and using whatever paint was available. **$45–$95**

CHAPTER NINE

Potpourri

Coffee grinder from early twentieth century.
$100–$125

During the course of a year we visit an antiques shop, show, mall, or market at least once a week over a wide geographic area. Our purposes are to add to our own collection and to monitor prices for the next edition of this book.

The task has become more complex in recent years as the number of shows, markets, and malls has increased significantly and the quality of merchandise available has decreased. We find that we now have to go much farther and go more often to locate items that even a decade ago were fairly common.

This chapter is devoted to a cross section of country antiques that were especially interesting to us during our travels.

Overpainted factory-made spice box. **$150–$175**

Factory-made spice box, early twentieth century. **$200–$225**

Factory-made metal spice box, original gold paint and black lettering on drawers. **$400–$500**

Spice box, original finish and drawer pulls, early 1900s. **$250–$300**

Refinished pine spice box, replaced drawer pulls. **$100–$115**

Factory-made staved "dasher" butter churn, stenciled label, original finish. **$225–$275**

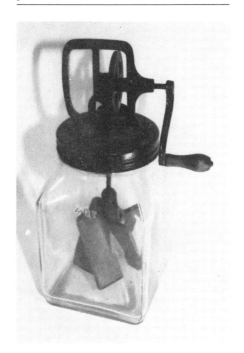

Glass "paddle" butter churn. **$45–$55**

Oak wall telephone, original finish, c. 1930. $175–$250

Butter churn with "piggin" handle and "buttonhole" hoops, painted finish. $475–$575

Coffee grinder, original finish, "as found" condition, c. 1870. $85–$100

Spice grinder, original finish, factory-made, c. 1880. $135–$150

Refinished coffee grinder, c. 1890. $95–$115

Coffee grinder from early twentieth century. $100–$125

Unusual coffee grinder with pillars, possibly European in origin. $75–$100

Factory-made coffee grinder, dovetailed, traces of original label. $115–$130

Painted coffee grinder, $115–$130; miniature coffee grinder, $35–$65.

Pine wall box, painted finish, late nineteenth century. **$175–$250**

Painted pine knife-and-fork box, late nineteenth century. **$85–$100**

Pine box, original painted finish. **$75–$100**

Knife-and-fork box, painted finish. **$150–$185**

Open utility box, pine, painted finish, nailed sides. **$75–$100**

Unusual knife-and-fork box with turned handle and lapped sides. **$150–$175**

Painted box, "Rose Lewis," pine, c. 1870. **$300–$375**

Decorated utility box, pine. **$55–$75**

Unusual rectangular box with iron handle, bracket base, and original finish. **$300–$375**

Painted pine box, 8″ × 4″ × 5″, nailed sides, nineteenth century. **$100–$125**

Pine ballot box, dovetailed sides, painted finish. **$125–$150**

Immigrant's box, originally from Norway, blue exterior and red interior, mid-nineteenth century. **$600–$750**

Dovetailed pine dough box, blue paint, splayed sides. **$350–$425**

Painted pine scouring box, nineteenth century. **$225–$250**

Hanging wall box, back section made from a cupboard door panel, yellow paint, 1880–1910. **$150–$175**

Leaf design on maple butter mold. **$75–$100**

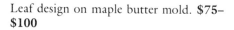

Painted pine carrier, iron handle, nailed sides. **$125–$150**

"Bird on a branch" butter print. **$275–$350**

"Strawberry and leaf" design on maple butter mold. **$135–$150**

Machine-stamped "cow" butter mold. **$300–$400**

Miniature butter mold, maple, refinished. **$45–$60**

American eagle butter stamp. **$450–$600**

"Wheat" butter print. **$125–$150**

"Double wheat" butter print. **$200–$275**

Hand-carved "heart" butter print. **$225–$250**

Butter mold with three leaves, maple. **$100–$125**

Shaker clothes brush, turned handle, late nineteenth century. **$135–$150**

Shaker-type brush, turned maple handle, original painted finish. **$45–$55**

Nineteenth-century paintbrush, maple handle. **$12–$15**

Broom-corn whisk broom, early 1900s. **$8-$12**

Broom-corn brush with maple handle, original blue paint. **$75–$85**

Broom-corn whisk broom, late nineteenth century. **$10–$15**

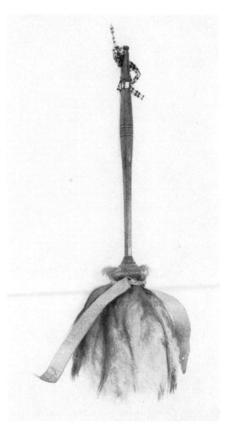

Shaker duster, original decorative yellow ribbon, turned maple handle. **$300–$350**

Whisk broom, broom corn, original blue paper holder, early 1900s. **$15–$20**

Shaker-type brush, turned and painted handle. **$45–$55**

Carved wooden kitchen paddle. **$15–$20**

Cranberry scoop, factory-made, early 1900s. **$200–$225**

Walnut washboard, factory-made, c. 1900. **$125–$175**

Maple rolling pins. **$25–$30** each

Unusual turned and painted rolling pin, original finish. **$55–$70**

Wooden washboards. **$45–$60** each

Turned maple rolling pin with painted handles, early 1900s. **$15–$20**

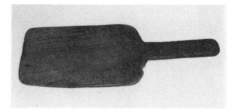

Peel used to take hot baked goods or plates from an oven, pine, unfinished, difficult to date. **$45–$55**

Crudely carved wooden spoon, possibly European in origin. **$45–$55**

Wooden scoop from a grocery store, made from a single piece of maple, late nineteenth century. **$135–$150**

Tiger maple butter worker. **$150–$225**

Meat pounder, turned maple, early twentieth century. **$20–$25**

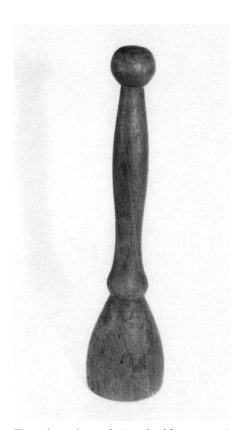

Hand-hewn wooden bowl, nineteenth century. **$135–$150**

Five wooden bowls, turned maple, painted finish. **$1000–$1200** set of five

Turned maple pestle (used with a mortar) for grinding spices or herbs, original finish, late nineteenth century. **$20–$28**

Staved wooden bucket, hickory bands, late nineteenth century. **$100–$125**

Turned wooden bowl and maple household utensils, early twentieth century: bowl, **$55**; butter worker, **$30–$35**.

Staved wooden sap bucket, painted finish, metal bands. $75–$85

Staved pail with bail or "drop" handle, metal bands, late nineteenth century. $75–$95

Bail-handled staved pail, painted finish, metal bands. $75–$95

Shaker pail, staved contruction, metal bands, painted finish, diamond brace on side, early twentieth century. $250–$275

Shaker milk keeler, painted finish, finger lap construction, pine staves, nineteenth century. **$600–$750**

Shaker pails, staved construction, painted finish: 4″ diameter, **$250–$275**; 6″ diameter, **$300–$350**.

Shaker oval boxes, maple and pine, copper nails, painted finish, 11″ and 14″ in length, nineteenth century. **$2000–$2500** each

Painted carrier, maple and pine, nineteenth century. **$135–$150**

Shaker measure in blue paint with finger lap, maple and pine. **$400–$500**

Painted sugar bucket or firken, factory-made, bail handle, late nineteenth century. **$225–$275**

Blue painted barrel, staved construction with metal bands, lift lid, early twentieth century. **$300–$350**

Painted firken, maple and pine, bail handle, buttonhole hoops. **$375–$450**

Blue barrel, iron handles, metal bands, staved construction. **$300–$350**

Shaker butter box, painted pine and maple, buttonhole hoops, nineteenth century. **$425–$500**

Painted pantry boxes with drop handles (bail handles). **$200–$225** each

Bail-handled pantry box, painted finish, factory-made. **$200–$225**

Cast iron cake mold, mid-nineteenth century. **$200–$225**

Painted firken or sugar bucket, unusually small size with 5″ diameter at base, factory-made, nineteenth century. **$300–$350**

Wrought iron toaster, c. 1840. **$300–$350**

Cast iron pump, early twentieth century. **$45–$55**

Iron scale, early twentieth century. **$75–$90**

Cast iron match holder, late nineteenth century. **$50–$60**

Miniature cast iron kettle with bail handle, c. 1900. **$150–$176**

Cast iron cooking pot, bail handle, early 1900s. **$50–$65**

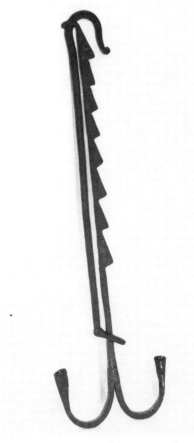

Wrought iron double trammel candle holder, American, early nineteenth century. **$600–$800**

Iron ice tongs for carrying blocks of ice, early 1900s. **$30–$35**

Cast iron kettle, bail handle, c. 1900. **$75–$85**

Cast iron scales, c. 1890. **$125–$150**

Cast iron muffin mold, c. 1900. **$50–$60**

Pine checkerboard, original painted surface, early 1900s. **$400–$450**

Rocking horse, late nineteenth century. **$700–$900**

Pine checkerboard, original painted surface, early 1900s. **$300–$375**

Much-loved rocking horse, late nineteenth century. **$500–$650**

Child's rocking chair, 1930s. **$200–$225**

Large birdhouse, original painted finish, c. 1950. **$75–$100**

Painted birdhouse found in Vermont, c. 1920. **$150–$175**

Simple birdhouse of indeterminate age, painted finish. **$35–$50**

Birdhouse with unusual roof, orignal painted finish, c. 1940. **$85–$100**

Unusual birdhouse with steps leading to opening, 1930s. **$100–$125**

257

Birdhouse church, 1950s. **$35–$50**

Goose decoy, original painted finish, 1930s.
$225–$275

Plane, nineteenth century. **$75–$90**

Plane, late nineteenth century. **$75–$90**

Cast iron snow eagle used to hold snow on roofs, late nineteenth century. **$100–$125**

Fire truck, original painted condition, late 1940s. **$2000–$2500**

Farm wagon, original condition, c. 1930. **$400–$500**

Blacksmith's bellows, 48″ long, painted red, early 1900s. **$325–$375**

Fire bell from Lincoln, Illinois, c. 1920. **$125–$140**

Chalkware cat, early twentieth century. **$200–$250**

Painted pine box used for "Mail," gold paint lettering, found in North Carolina, early 1900s. **$150–$175**

Painting of husband, wife, and dog, in period frame, c. 1850. **$500–$600**

Grained pine hanging cupboard, mid-nineteenth century. **$700–$850**

Governor weight made by the Flint and Walling Manufacturing Company of Kendallville, Indiana, c. 1900. **$225–$275**

Jukebox from the early 1940s, original veneered finish. **$500–$700**

Schoolhouse clock, c. 1900. **$300–$400**

"Barnacle-eye" windmill weight, made by the Elgin Wind Power and Pump Company of Elgin, Illinois, late nineteenth century. **$850–$1000**

Mantel clock, c. 1880. **$300–$400**

Southern Calendar Clock, St. Louis, Missouri, patent date of July 4, 1876. **$500–$600**

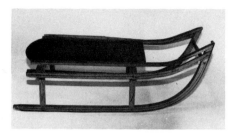

Child's sled, factory-made, early twentieth century. **$150–$175**

Halloween noisemaker, 1950s. **$10–$12**

Black doll, 1930s. **$125–$150**

Child's stove, c. 1930. **$200–$225**

Teddy bear, early 1940s. **$75–$100**

Log cabin dollhouse, 1930s. **$350–$450**

Horse-drawn wagon, c. 1940. **$65–$75**

Handcrafted Wabash Railroad Company #57 engine, 1930s. **$65–$75**

Pedal Trac tractor, c. 1960. **$175–$225**

Caboose, original painted finish, 1930s. **$100–$125**

Wicker baby buggy, 1940. **$100–$125**

Cardboard Christmas candy box, c. 1930. **$8–$10**

Wicker baby buggy, 1940s. **$125–$150**

Plastic Santa Claus, 14″ tall, c. 1950. **$50–$65**

Easter pull toy, cardboard, wooden base with metal wheels, c. 1940. **$35–$45**

Compressed-Cardboard Collectibles

From the 1930s through the 1950s the dime stores of America had shelves filled with Halloween jack-o'-lanterns and Easter bunnies to be used for decoration or to be filled with candy.

$55–$60

$40–$55

$50–$60

$55–$60

$50–$60

$45–$50

$60–$70

$200–$225

$40–$50

$175–$200

$100–$125

Country Baskets and Tinware

Unlike most segments of the country antiques market, baskets are especially difficult to date and evaluate. A contemporary basket maker uses the same materials and techniques that were followed a century earlier. A year of use and exposure can artificially age a splint basket significantly. Baskets were also utilitarian, and many contain breaks or cracked pieces of splint or are missing handles.

An "old" basket may also be 50 years old to be legitimately regarded as an "antique." Crudely made European imports and factory-made baskets held together with staples and nails are still common. Such baskets presently have minimal value but often carry substantial price tags in shops. Most antiques malls in America have an ample supply of factory-made baskets with machine-cut splint and staples and nails.

Old handcrafted country baskets should show obvious signs of use and have some patina. If the basket has been oiled or coated with some type of finish, the basket should be left on the seller's shelf and not added to a personal antiques collection.

Painted baskets are eagerly collected, and legitimate examples are extremely difficult to locate. The same care should be taken when examining and considering a painted basket as is taken when considering a piece of furniture with its "original" surface finish.

Baskets turn up at backyard estate auctions in Iowa almost as often as in Pennsylvania because a century ago every household had several. Generally they are under the basement steps or in a cupboard, filled with clothespins or other useful items.

Buttocks basket, rib construction, wrapped rim. **$140–$175**

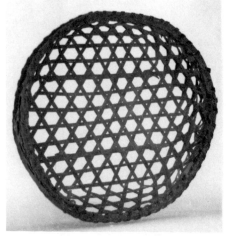

Cheese basket, 26″ diameter. **$600–$700**

White oak splint baskets, rib construction: average size, **$100–$125**; miniature, **$75–$100**.

Half-bushel basket, painted green. **$375–$500**

The quality of a handcrafted basket is obvious when such a basket is compared to a basket with machine-cut splint made in the early twentieth century. The handle of the handcrafted basket in the picture has been carved and notched through the basket rim and is held by wrapped splint.

Painted utility basket, carved handle, from New England. **$300–$350**

Gathering basket, rib construction, white oak splint. **$175–$225**

Painted and decorated miniature basket, carved handle, found in New York. **$450–$550**

Half basket, ash splint, rib construction. **$250–$300**

Twentieth-century basket of machine-cut splint held together by wire staples rather than splint. **$50–$65**

Splint knife-and-fork basket, painted green, carved handle. **$250–$300**

Storage basket for use on a table, wrapped rim, carved and notched handles. **$200–$225**

Indian-made comb basket, painted green, late nineteenth century. **$300–$350**

Factory-made sewing basket, twentieth century. **$75–$100**

Twentieth-century Easter basket, machine-cut splint. **$15–$25**

Gizzard basket, white oak splint. **$175–$225**

Tin measuring cup with pouring spout, late nineteenth century. **$20–$25**

Ice cream scoop, c. 1920. **$15–$18**

Child's lunch box, blue, c. 1910. **$25–$40**

Egg-sizing scale, c. 1930. **$15–$20**

Leather fire bucket, early 1800s. **$450–$550**

Food grater, c. 1940. **$15–$18**

Food graters: rare round grater, **$50–$65**; rectangular grater, **$30–$35**.

Chopping knife, early 1900s. **$20–$24**

Tin strainer, late nineteenth century. **$28–$35**

Tin milk can for carrying to school with lunch pail. **$45–$55**

Wick trimmer, mid-nineteenth century. **$50–$65**

Tole-painted wash bowl, c. 1850. **$125–$175**

Two-tube candle mold, rare form, c. 1850. **$150–$200**

Circular 12-tube candle mold, rare form, mid-nineteenth century. **$900–$1200**

Pierced-tin candle lantern, c. 1860. **$400–$500**

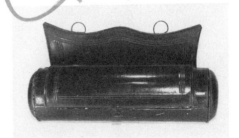

Tin candle box, painted black, c. 1860. **$375–$450**

Pewter saucer candle holder, possibly English, c. 1840. **$125–$150**

Indian-made storage basket, painted blue, used on a table or bureau. **$350–$425**

Cast Iron Trivets

From the middle of the nineteenth century through the first quarter of the twentieth century many American cities east of the Mississippi River had a local foundry that produced cast iron furnaces, tools, decorative fencing, wagon and train wheels, and household utensils. As a sideline, some of the foundries made cast iron trivets for local homemakers as Christmas gifts, for advertising, or for selling to mail-order operations like Montgomery Ward or Sears and Roebuck. The trivets were popular and necessary to keep hot irons and cooking pots from burning down the house. The trivets were made in a wide variety of shapes and sizes, with decorations ranging from geometrics to hearts and messages like "Good Luck to all who use this stand."

Left to right: $75–$85, $65–$75, $75–$85.

Trivet given to wives of veterans of the Confederate States of America in Richmond, Virginia, in the early 1900s at an annual convention. **$125–$175**

Left to right: **$75–$85, $75–$85, $55–$70**.

$75–$85

$75–$90

$50–$60

$135–$150

$50–$60

$50–$75

$75–$90

$75–$100

Iron. $30–$40

$75–$100

$135–$160

$75–$100

Iron. $30–$45

$75–$90

Iron. $30–$45

$55–$80

Glossary

Painted pine carrier, iron handle and nailed sides. **$125–$150**

If you are going to collect American country antiques, a working vocabulary of commonly used terms is a necessity. If you are not already conversant with the words that follow, study the definitions closely and look for what they represent at the next show, auction, or market you attend.

Collectors who pay a great deal of money for American country pieces should have some knowledge about the types of items they are seeking. Dealers are often accustomed to conducting business with individuals who don't have a clue about what they are buying. Customers who have a basic understanding of phrases and terms in daily use in the antiques business normally are taken much more seriously than is the casual tire kicker whose grandmother had three or four of everything in the booth or shop.

apron (skirt) Portion of a table directly below the top that is fastened to the top and supports the legs. Can be very simple or highly decorative.

architectural Typically refers to a case piece (such as a cupboard or chest of drawers) that was originally built into a home, rather than a piece of freestanding furniture that could be moved around at will. Should show a lack of wear and finish on at least one side (the one that would have been in contact with a wall or corner).

as found (as is) A piece of furniture that has recently come out of a barn or basement and has not been refinished, reworked, or refined can be described as "as found."

attribution A term used to describe or document that a particular individual was probably the maker of a piece of country furniture (or some other item) because few were actually signed.

blind front A blind-front cupboard has solid upper doors with no glass. Blind front is the opposite of a "glazed" front.

breadboard ends Thin strips of wood attached to the ends of a table top to keep the top from warping over time.

burl A growth or knob found on the sides of hardwood trees that was finely sliced and used as a decorative veneer or was hollowed out and used as a bowl.

case piece A piece of furniture that is framed like a box. Examples are cupboards, desks, and chests of drawers. The carcase of a case piece is the frame with any drawers or doors taken off.

commode A small case piece, often made of a softwood, designed to hold a pitcher and bowl set on its top and a chamber pot in an enclosed area below. Many were factory-made in the 1870–1900 period. A washstand is similar to a commode in purpose but does not have an enclosed area below.

container furniture A negative term used to describe furniture purchased in Europe by the shipping container full. The furniture is typically of low quality and is reworked, reproduced, or recycled.

crest rail The top slat of a chair. On kitchen chairs the crest rail was often decorated by brush or stencil.

dovetail A woodworker's technique used to join two pieces of wood at a corner. Often found on nineteenth-century chests of drawers. Can be done by hand or stamped out by machine (after 1890).

Empire A style of furniture that was very popular in the United States from the 1820s through the early 1850s (and longer in some rural areas).

escutcheon A protective round or oval plate (made of wood, brass, ivory, or porcelain) positioned around a keyhole.

finial A decorative or ornamental turning on the top of the back posts of a chair or the four posts of a bed.

glazed A piece of furniture that is glazed has glass in it. A glazed-front cupboard has upper doors with panes of glass.

graining A technique done with paint and brush commonly employed to make a softwood (pine or poplar) case piece or box appear to be of a more exotic or desirable wood (such as cherry, walnut, oak, or mahogany). This technique was especially popular in the late nineteenth century, during which time large quantities of woodwork and doors in homes and furniture was grained or painted to resemble oak. Often a piece of furniture is considerably older than its coat of grained paint.

"light" An individual pane of glass, often found in the upper portion of a cupboard. A glazed-front cupboard with eight panes of glass is said to have eight "lights."

married Generally the unhappy mating of two individual pieces of furniture that share some similar design characteristics. For example, the bottom of a cupboard may be paired with the upper portion of another cupboard to form an "original" piece of furniture. Furniture is married more often to deceive rather than to enhance.

overpaint Term used to describe several coats of paint on top of an original painted surface. Generally a negative term which suggests that a piece will have to be carefully stripped one coat at a time to have any value; however, this is not always true, as many overpainted pieces are still exceptional pieces of country furniture in "as found" condition and need no work.

patina The surface appearance of a piece of furniture (or other item), caused by exposure to time, dust, human contact, weather, and periodic bumps and bruises.

picker An individual who spends a great deal of time at auctions, at tag and home sales, and on the road in search of merchandise ("merch") to sell to other dealers. Primarily a wholesaler whose primary mission is to move his or her product through sales to a regular list of dealers. A picker could be described as a "dealer's dealer."

pieced out Chairs and tables often have to have several inches added to their legs to raise them to a more desirable modern height. This process is called piecing out. If a chair or table is refinished, the change is usually fairly obvious; however, if the paint on the new addition is matched to the original paint on the leg, it can create some identification problems.

primitive A term in general use in the 1950s through 1970s used to describe what is now called "country."

provenance This term generally refers to the history of ownership of a particular piece. In most cases it is extremely difficult to trace the history of a piece accurately unless it has stayed in a single family for its entire life.

"right" A cupboard that is "right" is exactly what it is advertised to be. This term suggests that no alterations or structural changes have been made to a piece. A chair that has been pieced out could not be described as "right."

score marks Marks made on chairs and bedposts to indicate where slats, rungs, or head and foot boards could go.

scribe marks Marks made on drawers to indicate depth of dovetails. Drawers with scribe marks indicate that the work was done by hand rather than stamped out by machine.

scrubbed Term used to describe a softwood tabletop that has literally been scrubbed so many times that the paint has worn off, leaving a grayish-white surface that results from contact with soap and water.

skinned A piece of furniture that has been refinished to the point that any trace of "old" is gone. "Skinned" is a negative term used to describe a piece that has been sanded "to death."

"smalls" A term used by dealers to de-

scribe items that can be easily packed and transported to and from antiques shows (i.e., not furniture).

stretcher (rung) A piece of wood (usually turned on a lathe) that connects and serves as a brace for the legs of a chair or table. A rung is always turned and serves as a stretcher on a chair.

till A small hinged box found inside a blanket chest.

treen Having to do with wooden kitchen or hearth utensils; woodenware.

turn button A carved piece of wood used to hold a cupboard door closed when the wooden piece is turned horizontally. Often held to a case piece by a screw.

turned Chair legs and posts and bedposts were generally shaped, or turned, on a lathe.

veneer A thinly cut strip of wood glued to a piece of furniture to give the impression of a more desirable kind of wood.

Victorian Name given to several styles of heavy, factory-made walnut furniture popular from about 1850 until the early 1900s. Also refers to anything made in the ornate style popular during this period.

Tenth Anniversary Edition of the Nefarious Final Exam

Bail-handled staved pail, painted finish, metal bands. **$75–95**

Introduction

This is the tenth examination that we have compiled. Questions have been secured from selected antiques dealers, K Mart home furnishings managers, and two cosmetologists from Los Gatos, California.

All of the questions have been carefully evaluated and chosen on the basis of their difficulty and geographic impartiality. Any rumors that you have read in the *Used Car Weekly* or *Swine News* about these test results being occasionally sanctioned by a jukebox repair school in Bayonne, New Jersey, are probably untrue.

Your score will be posted in the gymnasium on Friday or Wednesday. If it is not posted, hesitate to call.

Directions

1. Memorize the directions before you begin. They will not be repeated. You will not be allowed to refer back to the test manual for assistance.
2. Do not stop until you have completed the examination.

3. Find someone other than a relative to pick up the official answer sheet. It is critical that the person *not* be a former resident of a state penal institution, an employee of a carnival or real estate agency, or an attorney.
4. The official answer sheet is a regular supplement to several weekly newspapers on sale near you.
5. Do *not* ask for help unless the situation is life-threatening.

1. This is a .

2. It originally came from a
   a. private home
   b. grocery store
   c. a and b are equally correct

3. It is made of
   a. a combination of metals
   b. cast aluminum
   c. wrought iron
   d. cast iron

4. What is its approximate age?

5. The wooden handle is made of
   a. maple
   b. pine
   c. walnut
   d. ash

6. It has an approximate value of more than $200 but less than $600.
   true   false

7. This is a _____ cupboard.
   a. step-back
   b. drop front
   c. seventeenth century
   d. all of the above
   e. none of the above

8. The approximate value of the cupboard is greater than $3000.
   true   false

9. This cupboard dates from the _____ quarter of the nineteenth century.
   a. first
   b. second
   c. third
   d. fourth
   e. none of the above

10. These crocks were decorated with a
_____.
   a. slip cup
   b. brush
   c. stencil
   d. broom

11. The *total* value of the three crocks
   is
   a. $200–$300
   b. $500–$600
   c. more than $600

12. It is obvious from the form and
   decoration that these pieces were
   made in Illinois, Indiana, or Ohio
   around 1850.
   true   false

13. This painted pie safe is worth *at
   least* $1200.
   true   false

14. How would you date this pie safe?
   a. before 1830
   b. 1830–1850
   c. 1860–1880
   d. after 1900

15. It almost certainly is *not* made of
   a. walnut
   b. pine
   c. poplar
   d. oak

16. Which color below would make it
   the most desirable?
   a. brown
   b. yellow
   c. black
   d. white

17. *Refinished*, the pie safe would be
   worth approximately
   a. $300
   b. $800
   c. $1500
   d. $2200

18. This dry sink is *probably* made of
    a. cherry
    b. walnut
    c. oak
    d. pine

19. Which of the four woods below would be the *least* desirable?
    a. cherry
    b. walnut
    c. oak
    d. pine

20. This dry sink dates from approximately
    a. 1740–1780
    b. 1800–1830
    c. 1840–1850
    d. after 1860

21. If it were painted yellow and in "as found" condition, what would be its approximate value?
    a. $300–$500
    b. $600–$700
    c. $750–$850
    d. $1200–$1400

22. Factory-made dry sinks were often constructed of cherry or tiger maple.
    true   false

23. *Check* the terms below that best describe this jar.
    ____ redware
    ____ stoneware
    ____ molded
    ____ "thrown"
    ____ c. 1830
    ____ c. 1900
    ____ handcrafted
    ____ mass-produced
    ____ cobalt-decorated
    ____ Bristol glaze

24. The value of this jar *without* a paper label would be reduced by at least 50 percent.
    true   false

25. This jar would be worth less than a stenciled canning jar from the Hamilton & Jones Pottery of Greensboro, Pennsylvania.
    true   false

26. These rolling pins date from the nineteenth century.
    true   false

27. Rolling pins can be found made of
    a. wood
    b. stoneware
    c. glass
    d. a and b
    e. all of the above

28. The two rolling pins are made of
    _____.
    a. oak
    b. ash
    c. pine
    d. none of the above

29. If you handed the clerk in an antiques shop a $400 bill, approximately how much change would you get back when you bought the two rolling pins?
    a. $85
    b. $160
    c. $300
    d. you would be arrested or institutionalized for trying to pass a $400 bill

30. Most factory-made woodenware is made of _____.

31. This bowl was turned on a lathe.
    true   false

32. It is a burl bowl.
    true   false

33. The rocking horse would date from
    a. prior to 1900
    b. about 1940
    c. 1900–1920

34. Its current value is approximately
    a. less than $100
    b. $200–$225
    c. $400–$500
    d. more than $500

35. The Country Antiques Hall of Fame is located in Belden, Nebraska, at 103 East Grant Court.

true   false

36. An overpainted cupboard would bring less money than an otherwise identical cupboard that had been "skinned."

true   false

Essay Question (10 points)

Discuss in detail the west-to-north migration patterns of early twentieth-century antiques collectors in relation to the price structure of cupboards and cupolas in Cleveland, Columbus, Chicago, and Coffeyville. Include in your answer specific references to Stanley Coveleski, Trini Lopez, and the movement to reunite the farm workers from Samoa with Freddy and the Dreamers.

Answers

1. coffee grinder
2. b
3. d
4. 1875–1910
5. a
6. true
7. a
8. false
9. d
10. b
11. c
12. false: Pennsylvania
13. true
14. c
15. d
16. b
17. b
18. d
19. c
20. d
21. d
22. false: oak or combinations of several woods
23. stoneware, molded, c. 1900, mass-produced, Bristol glaze
24. true
25. true
26. true
27. e
28. d (correct answer is maple)
29. d
30. maple
31. true
32. false
33. b
34. b
35. false
36. false

Scoring Scale

45–50   A scholarship in your name will be established in the mouthwash or leisure wear section of any department store of your choosing in Altoona, Pennsylvania.

39–44   Once your score has been certified you will receive a free pass to any Lash LaRue motion picture in your hometown in July. You must bring your own whip and black hat or be accompanied by Guy Madison, Duncan Renaldo, or one of their designated representatives.

33–38   The president of your high school senior class has been notified about your score, and he or she was disgusted with your ignorance. At the next reunion everyone will know and be equally ashamed. Any

mention of you as a member of the Pep Club will be expunged from the yearbook.

less than 38   You may never use or learn the secret grip or password at antiques shops to get the special discount awarded members of our "Great Achievement" group.